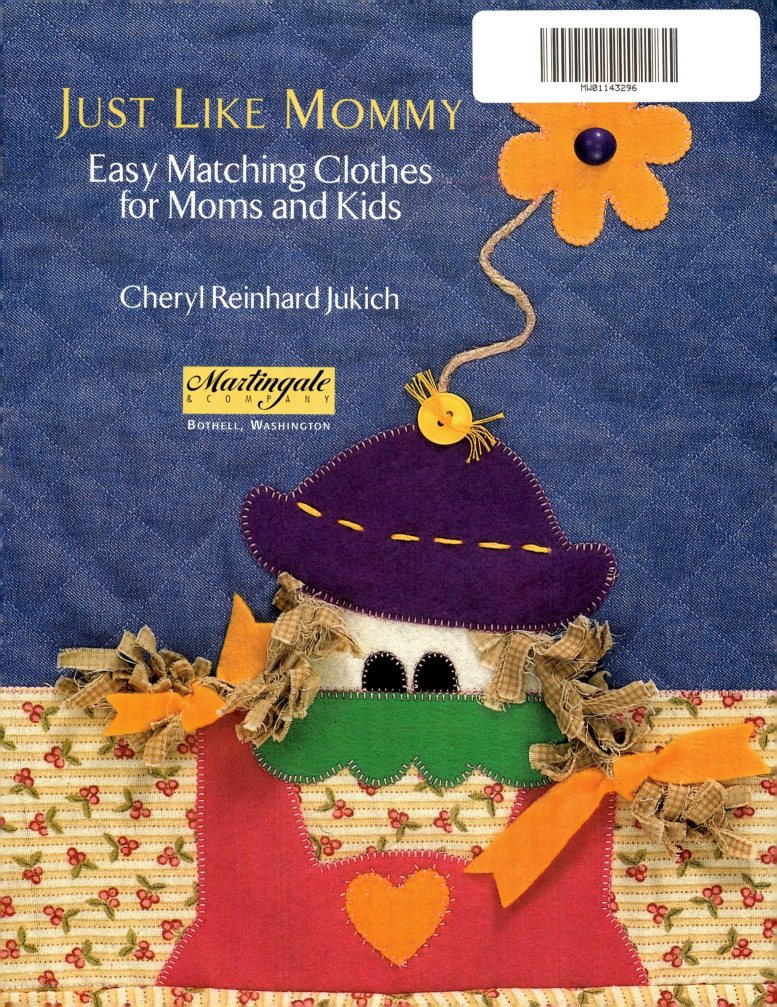

JUST LIKE MOMMY

Easy Matching Clothes
for Moms and Kids

Cheryl Reinhard Jukich

Martingale
& COMPANY
BOTHELL, WASHINGTON

Credits

President . . . . Nancy J. Martin
CEO/Publisher . . . . Daniel J. Martin
Associate Publisher . . . . Jane Hamada
Editorial Director . . . . Mary V. Green
Technical Editor . . . . Darra Williamson
Design and Production
Manager . . . . Cheryl Stevenson
Cover and Text Designer . . . . Stan Green
Copy Editor . . . . Liz McGehee
Illustrator . . . . Laurel Strand
Photographer . . . . Brent Kane

That Patchwork Place, Inc., is an imprint of
Martingale & Company.

Just Like Mommy: Easy Matching Clothes for Moms and Kids
© 1999 by Cheryl Reinhard Jukich

Martingale & Company,
PO Box 118, Bothell, WA 98041-0118 USA

Library of Congress Cataloging-in-Publication Data
Jukich, Cheryl Reinhard.
    Just like mommy : easy matching clothes for moms and kids /
Cheryl Reinhard Jukich.
        p. cm.
    ISBN 1-56477-277-2
    1. Clothing and dress. 2. Children's clothing 3. Machine quilting
Patterns. I. Title.
TT560.J85 1999
746.46' 0432—dc21   99-21044
                                                 CIP

Printed in Hong Kong
04 03 02 01 00 99   6 5 4 3 2 1

MISSION STATEMENT

We are dedicated to providing quality
products and service by working together
to inspire creativity and to enrich the
lives we touch.

DEDICATION

To my sister, Gail Reinhard Mikesell,
for courage, grace, and laughter
under the line of life's fire. You are
truly an inspiration!

THANK YOU!

So many wonderful people to thank, but so little
space left!

When you work on a project of this magnitude,
there are so many people who help make it happen,
and most of them remain unrecognized for their "devo-
tion to the cause." To those mentioned below and
others: Bless you.

First, I thank God for the talent He has bestowed
on me, and pray that I continue to use it wisely.

Many, many "thank-you" hugs to my husband, Bill,
for the loads of clean laundry, the vacuumed carpets, and
general househusbandry while I work late at the office,
not only for this book, but for the many projects the
company is involved in. What a treat to come home to
the aroma of a tasty meal, or to have a mug of hot,
steamy tea magically appear as I work late into the
night.

Thanks also to my parents, Ann and Paul Reinhard,
for indulging my artistic fantasies as a child—and for
continuing to do so. See! All of those paint sets, pastels,
and coloring books weren't wasted!

And then there is Mary Green, editorial director at
Martingale and Company, whose patience and under-
standing have guided me through the peaks and valleys
of going solo. I owe her a year's worth of Lady Clairol
to cover up the gray.

Gratitude as well to members of my outstanding
office staff who field calls, fetch lunches, and just keep
the place running while my mind is off in the clouds
designing.

I can't forget my trusty sewing assistant, Denise
Mendes, who meets my deadlines, never complains about
the workload that piles up on short notice, and who
operates a mean seam ripper. Thank you, thank you!

Add to the list my wonderful siblings, siblings-in-
law, and various and assorted relatives who always lend
an ear, inquire about progress, and sometimes brain-
storm with me. Y'all are the best!

And finally, thank you to my granddaughter, Emily
Clifton, age 7, for just making me laugh. My heart
bursts with joy when I look at her and her beautiful
artwork. Emily, I'm holding a place open for you at The
Threadbare Pattern Co.

CONTENTS

THE PROJECTS

WELCOME!

Dear Stitching and Crafting Friends,

Welcome to *Just Like Mommy*, my first solo book! Although I have contributed chapters to several other books over the years, this is my first individual effort, and I thank you, thank you, *thank you* for your support.

Splashed over these pages, you'll find fun new fabrics, such as fleece and shaggy plush felt showcased in garments that use fusible appliqué, twine embellishments, free-motion machine quilting, and my own Quik-Quilt™ techniques. The designs are simple to stitch, with many using fabric scraps and other bits and pieces that you probably already have in your craft and sewing stash. You don't need a fancy new machine—although that could be on your next holiday wish list!—or any special doodads to complete these projects.

My desire is for you to use this book as a stepping-stone to try new things, and to develop your confidence and creativity. While it is the ultimate compliment to me when you make one of my projects to the letter, I urge you to experiment with the colors, rearrange the appliqués, or add and subtract motifs to achieve your own personal look. Don't be afraid to think "off the bolt," as I like to say. I truly believe that you can use these projects as a jumping-off point to showcase your own personal vision.

Don't let lack of confidence deter you from attempting new projects and techniques. I will let you in on a little secret: Designers like me have racks of clothing and piles of projects that once showed the promise of greatness. Because vision does not always translate into reality, however, these projects will most likely never see the light of day. You are not alone!

The point is to choose a project, infuse it with your sense of style, relax, create . . . and have fun!

Happy stitching!

Cheryl Reinhard Jukich

The Threadbare Pattern Company ... and Me!

I guess I should have known I was pointed in the right direction when, as a young teen, I found myself in high demand in the fast-paced, high-finance world of my first career: babysitting! Yes, I was good with children (I have five extraordinarily creative siblings), but what kept the mothers dialing my number was the fact that I always brought my craft box along on the job. The kids *loved* it! Sometimes we made Popsicle-stick dolls or houses, or some masterpiece out of yarn or string. We might cut out doll clothes, or do something with pipe cleaners to keep the boys out of mischief. Just folding a piece of colored paper could be exciting, too!

Of course, as I aged, I chose to "retire" from babysitting and turned away from teaching others the fine art of crafting. I focused on boys, basketball games, decorating my room with objets d'art crafted from my dad's workshop, and creating "designer dresses" for important social engagements from my mom's fabric stash. The foundation for my future was being laid.

As an older teen, I discovered I really liked the idea of transforming the personality of a room by changing this or that, moving furniture here or there, or making a little something from nothing. I was on a roll, and when my folks let me apply the then-new technique of antiquing furniture to my own frumpy—I thought!—bed and vanity, a new career interest emerged.

College brought studies in interior design . . . and real life. Sewing and crafting faded into the background, but only temporarily. Nothing revives the crafter in a person more quickly than marriage and one's own nest to feather. When my parents asked what I would like for a wedding gift, I answered "a sewing machine," and they lovingly obliged. (I'm not sure that is the gift my husband would have chosen!) That wonderful sewing machine traveled the country far and wide. I was a military wife, and my love of sewing and crafting helped me change the atmosphere of many a dreary dwelling into a cozy refuge. Before long, it was helping me to make Raggedy Ann and Andy bumper pads, then little flannel "jammies," and later outfits for the first day of school for my two little darlings.

Fast forward on the tape of life. The little sewing machine has been replaced by several; The Threadbare Pattern Company was created in 1990; my husband has retired; and we now call North Carolina home. The little darlings are grown, and the best granddaughter in the world, little Emily, is showing artistic promise.

My life is filled with the love and friendship of a wide circle of family and friends, many of whom have contributed to the success of Threadbare Patterns. Starting as a custom appliqué jumper business, it quickly outgrew its humble attic surroundings. I'm not sure that the growth had as much to do with my business savvy as with the startling accumulation of fabric and my abundance of ideas. But whatever the reason, I soon outgrew my at-home space. It was a good feeling to have an office building from which to hang the Threadbare shingle. I still get a "warm fuzzy" when I drive past that little office on my way to the one we now occupy, and my landlord can't believe I've managed to fill *this* one up, too!

Through the years, much has changed, yet much has stayed the same. The original jumper patterns have been retired, and many new items have taken their place on our order form. Orders come from around the world, and with them an international base of customers, distributors, and new friends. My suitcases stay packed *up* more than packed *away*. And it's been the time of my life!

As I design, write, and teach, it's my wish that you unlock the creativity that God has given you. (I know it's within you . . . you've just got to work it, friends!) Don't let insecurity about choice of color, trims, or decorative stitches detour you from your creative journey. Who knows? I could soon be reading about *you!*

As for that wedding-gift sewing machine, it had so much sentimental value, I couldn't let it go. It now resides in the bedroom of my talented niece Nicks, who with her equally talented sister, Kate, sew up another generation's special-occasion "designer dresses."

Techniques, Terminology, and Tips

I hope you'll find the following basic information about materials and techniques helpful. I suggest you read through this section—and come back to it as necessary—as you begin the projects in this book. I've divided the information by category for easy reference.

Cheryl's Tips for Laundry Day

I think we wash our clothes to death! Now, I am not advocating walking around with ring-around-the-collar, and of course, in the event of an accident (heaven forbid!), you will want fresh undies on . . . but unless you have overturned your plate of spaghetti onto your lap, there is no reason to throw that jumper into the wash after one or two wearings. Hang it up to air out and lightly press as needed.

Detergent and the normal machine washing cycle are hard on your beautiful clothing. When you have taken your valuable time and talent to make and embellish a garment, you want it to last. The best way to do this is to limit, within reason, the number of washings. When you do need to launder the garment, use a mild detergent. I don't have a particular favorite, but I am sure you have one on hand. (Ivory Flakes comes to mind.) The important thing is to use any soap sparingly and use your washer's delicate cycle.

After you have washed the garment, don't just throw it into the dryer on "fry." Gently shake out the garment and place it in the dryer. Use the dryer's delicate or air cycle. When the garment is almost dry, take it out, finger-press any puckered seams, and hang it or lay it out on a towel to complete the drying. For cottons and flannels, a light touch-up with the iron will most likely be necessary. (We want to look nice, don't we?) Felts and Berbers shouldn't need touch-up ironing unless a lining is puckered along a seam.

Dry cleaning can be hard on clothing, too, so avoid it if at all possible. To be safe, always check the fabric manufacturers' instructions for their recommendations.

Fabrics, Supplies, and Notions

All the fabrics used in this book are widely available, relatively inexpensive, and easy to care for. All can be machine washed and dried. When purchasing any fabric, it's helpful to do a quick check of the information listed on each bolt end. You never know what kind of interesting information you might discover. And please let your local quilt- or fabric-store staff assist you if you have any questions. These ladies (and men) travel to trade shows, read sewing-related publications, and talk with fabric/notions representatives on a regular basis. They are eager to share their information. Remember, the only dumb question is the one that's not asked!

Berber: I think of this fun fabric as the "sophisticated" city cousin to fleece. And though it might have a sophisticated look, it isn't fussy in the sewing or care department. Like fleece, there are no edges to unravel, and it pops in the washer and dryer. I use this fabric when I want my garment to have a bit more panache, as you will see in my Fleece 'n Flannel jackets. The texture has a soft, nubby feel, which combines wonderfully with all the beautiful colors and prints that the manufacturers are producing. At your local fabric store, you will see lovely muted plaids with coordinating prints just waiting to be made into a cozy jacket or an upscale lap robe. And let's not stop with garments. This fabric would be equally at home as great north woods–style slipcovers, drapes, swags . . . the possibilities are endless.

Cotton/Reproduction Prints: You've probably heard the term "reproduction print" mentioned a few times in the last few years. What started out as a tribute to the much-treasured look of 1930s fabrics has whipped designers like me into a frenzy. Now you can see these beautiful 100%-cotton fabrics reproduced from textiles, not only of the '30s but also of the '40s and '50s, in colors and prints that will have you reminiscing about your lost youth! For example, the tablecloth fabric of the '50s on which we ate many a pot-roast dinner is being reproduced. (You know—the bright colors with the fruits.) It would make a terrific garden jacket! Since it's cotton, it is easy to care for, though you will need to plug in that iron once in awhile. But it's worth it, because nothing beats the feel of crisp, freshly ironed cotton fabric.

Craft Felt: Is there anyone out there who hasn't picked up a piece of craft felt and used it for a project? Surely not! It comes in squares, in yardage on a bolt, in a rainbow of colors, and—you may not realize this—it's washable and—hold on to your pincushion—dryable! Check the bolt next time and see if it doesn't say just that. If you haven't used plain ol' felt in awhile, try it the next time you need a simple appliqué shape. I think you will be pleasantly surprised.

Denim: There's always a perfect person in the crowd—and so it is with denim fabric. Even when it is worn thin, you can patch it or throw an appliqué over the hole, and it looks great again. You can wash it to death—contrary to my laundry tips above—and even iron it over and over again, yet it always retains its character.

Flannel: Remember when flannel went to bed with us every night in the form of a diaper, our jammies, or sometimes both? Then it slowly went out of favor in the sewing room, unless we were whipping up receiving blankets. However, some enterprising quilter—bless you, whoever you are!—decided that quilting could be even more exciting with flannel. A walk around your fabric store today shows hundreds of yards of soft, cuddly cotton flannel in more patterns, prints, and colors than you could ever use. Of course, it still makes a great pair of jammies, but jackets, jumpers, and vests all look stunning in fabulous flannel.

Fleece: Fleece is the "country cousin" to Berber (see page 6). You've seen this '90s fabric everywhere, especially if you live in the colder climes. It comes in loads of fun prints and bright colors, is lightweight but cozy to wear. There are fleece hats, scarves, garments, sheets—I even saw a stool slipcovered in it! I am sure you can add a few good ideas to the list. Unlike Berber with its nubby look, fleece has a smooth texture. Many times, though, these two fabric names are used interchangeably.

Plush Felt: This cool fabric is the "big sister" to shaggy plush felt by order of birth! It has a wonderful soft, smooth nap, comes in a wonderful variety of colors, and works equally well for stuffed animals and apparel.

Shaggy Plush Felt: This wonderful fuzzy fabric is reminiscent of the cuddly, old teddy bears and soft stuffed bunnies you cherished in your childhood. It is readily available, easy-care, wears and handles well, and is simple to work with.

Always prewash shaggy plush felt before beginning your project. Follow the manufacturer's guidelines for the recommended water temperature, cycle, detergent, and so on. Washing tightens the fabric's backing, and "explodes" the fibers on the front to give the plush the ultimate fuzzy look. Toss the laundered fabric in the dryer, remove it, and you are ready to cut and sew.

Be sure to clean the lint traps on your washer and dryer every time you launder shaggy plush felt. The fluffy fibers leave a bit of a mess behind, but the results are well worth this slight inconvenience.

Vintage Fabrics: Vintage fabrics can include anything from a panel of Granny's beautiful lace curtains to a bit of leftover flannel that you used for Buster's jammies twenty years ago. Of course, the term is relative. What one person considers true "vintage" is another crafter's stash, so use your best judgment when adding a vintage piece of fabric or trim to your project. Is the vintage piece beyond saving? Would it have more worth or usefulness if you incorporated it into a garment or quilt? Could a reproduction print substitute just as well? Ponder a bit before you take the scissors to anything that has special sentimental or true antique value.

A *word of caution here:* Product and brand names for shaggy plush felt and plush felt can be quite similar. Read package labels carefully when you shop, so you don't come home with the wrong product.

Batting: Many types of thin craft battings are available; we all have our favorites. For the projects in this book, I used Warm & Natural needled cotton batting because it gives just a bit of puff to the quilting. I often use it to add dimension to a collar or pocket as in "Winter Blessings" (page 22). You may prewash, following the manufacturer's instructions, if desired, though it isn't necessary for the projects. This batting is widely available in many sizes at most quilt and fabric shops. If *you* have a favorite brand that has similar properties, it's okay to use that brand.

Decorative Threads: Don't ever skimp on thread quality! Five for a dollar gives you five-for-a-dollar stitching. I know it's tempting to fill the shopping basket with a bargain, but save that thrift for canned tomato sauce! There are many quality thread manufacturers, so experiment and note your favorites. For everyday sewing and garment construction, I prefer Mettler cotton silk finish threads. They're made from Egyptian long-fiber cotton and stand up to my machine as it's racing along at Mach 2. For special machine-embroidery touches, I use Mettler's silky rayon threads. These are just my particular favorites, so don't let me steer you away from other quality threads that you have used successfully.

Dressmaker's Curve: This is a wonderful measuring tool for figuring out the sizing of necklines and armholes when making dresses. But since you won't be doing any "real" dressmaking in this book, you will be using the tool for rounding the edges of some of the jacket fronts. Don't despair if you don't already own a dressmaker's curve—simply run to the kitchen and grab a luncheon plate to use as a template! It gives the same results.

Embroidery Floss: As you read through the projects in this book, you'll discover many references to the use of embroidery floss. The reason is simple: it's my favorite thread! It comes in a

rainbow of wonderful colors and is available just about everywhere. Unless otherwise stated, use the floss "full strength"; that is, thread the needle with *all* the strands.

Fusible Web: There are many quality brands of fusible web available. The Warm Company, who also manufactures the Warm & Natural batting, has a wonderful product called Steam-A-Seam 2 appliqué sheets. It comes in craft-sheet packages as well as yardage. The beauty of this product is that after fusing one side of the webbing to your chosen fabric, tracing the desired shape, and removing the paper backing, you can temporarily bond the appliqué to the project. This helps when you aren't sure of the final placement and want to rearrange the appliqué pieces without scattering or shifting them. The package gives all the important details for use.

Steam-A-Seam 2 is also a "sewable" fusible, which means that after you permanently bond it to your project, it will not gum up and ruin your machine needle when you add a decorative stitch. This is very important! If you are new to fusing or have had this trouble with your current brand, please recheck the label and make sure you are using a sewable fusible.

Hook-and-Loop Fastener: This fastening method is commonly referred to by the brand name "Velcro." I refer to it as hook-and-loop fastener, which is the generic term. There are several brands available, all of which give satisfactory results; however, Velcro now offers a soft and flexible product that is especially wonderful when used as a clothing fastener.

Jute Twine: When a project calls for jute twine, you'll need just ordinary household twine. Use medium size if you have it. If you need to shop for it, try the hardware department of your local home-improvement store or variety store. Don't give up too quickly if your initial search is unsuccessful. Be diligent in your sleuthing! I have been known to find twine in the fishing section of the sporting-goods department, hidden in the housewares area, and—imagine this!—in the craft department.

Porcelain Buttons: If you are familiar with the Threadbare Pattern line, you already know that I am crazy about porcelain buttons. They are gorgeous, adding those special little touches that call

When attaching buttons with floss, leave the floss tails showing on the top side of the button after you make the knot. This adds a whimsical, 3-dimensional touch to the finished project.

attention to your needlework. I'll admit they can be pricey, but what color and realism they bring to your project!

Although porcelain buttons can be fragile, you can make them removable. Some companies even offer covers to protect them at laundry time. Check with your local quilt shop for their recommendations.

Rag Fringe: This neat little trim is produced and sold by my great friends at Cotton Way in Idaho (see "Resources" on page 95). I thought it was the greatest when I first saw it at a trade show, and begged for samples so I could experiment. It is made from yards and yards of folded fabric, cut into fringe, and washed to make it all curly and squiggly. It's available in lots of colors and makes a great embellishment for pockets as well as for beards, hair, and my fringe flowers. It's all cotton, so it's easy to work with. You must give this a try!

Special Machine Attachments: While you don't need lots of special attachments to accomplish the stitches I recommend, these two might make life easier for you, particularly when machine quilting.

The *walking foot* attachment keeps multiple layers of fabric from shifting as they are guided over the feed dogs of your machine. Use it for cross-hatching or any other straight-line quilting tasks (see "Crosshatch Quilting" on page 19).

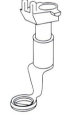

Walking Foot

The *darning foot* is ideal for free-motion machine quilting. That's the little round circle foot that you've probably never used. (Guess you haven't been darning socks lately!) The round circle acts as a little hoop that keeps the fabric under control while the needle is doing its thing. Most every sewing machine comes with one. Check to see if you have one, and refer to your manual for any specific settings required by your manufacturer.

Darning Foot

Spray Starch: I love spray starch! Nothing makes cutting easier, stitching smoother, or the finished garments look crisper and fresher than a shot of spray starch and a hot iron. Stock up on an inexpensive brand, and when my instructions call for a "press," give that block or seam a little squirt. You might be so pleased, you'll start ironing your linens again!

Water-Soluble Marker: This marker usually contains "Carolina blue" or purple ink that, with a squirt of water, magically disappears. Use caution! There are many markers on the market and all work well for particular purposes; just make sure your purpose and the marker's are the same! Many a gal has picked up and used a disappearing marking pen by mistake, to discover the next day that the marks had vanished. Not a pretty sight! Pay close attention to the marking pen you are purchasing. Read the manufacturer's guidelines on the package so you won't be disappointed.

Sometimes water-soluble ink can be a bit stubborn and comes back after you have squirted it. Just squirt again until the ink is truly gone.

Yarn: I am referring to any thin, fuzzy, or knobby yarn that can be used for doll hair. There are many types, styles, and brands on the market, and you can use any of them as long as the fiber is thin enough to poke through the holes of a button and strong enough so it will not shred when you tie knots. Speak with your sewing-shop staff to see what they offer and recommend.

Selecting and Preparing a Sweatshirt

Several projects in the book use my Quik-Quilt™ technique. This method always starts with a sweatshirt. The sweatshirt serves as your pattern piece, the batting, and—in most cases—the lining for the finished garment. When you are through, you will have a garment that looks like a soft, cuddly old quilt, without having to destroy a true treasure.

SELECTING A SWEATSHIRT

Please pay particular attention to the type and style of sweatshirt that is listed in the materials list of the individual project. It *will* make a difference in the quality of your project.

First let's talk about types and brands. There are two types of sweatshirts on the shelves today:

the raglan and set-in sleeve. Both are shown below. I always specify a set-in sleeve sweatshirt because I want a "real" sleeve to take off and embellish. Besides, I think they are more flattering than the raglan variety with that seam pointing right up to your neck. Ugh! When you are buying several sweatshirts at a time (to stock up for projects, of course) please, please double-check each one to make sure it has set-in sleeves. There have been times when I arrived home to find that a raglan sleeve had jumped in my bag because I was paying attention only to size and color and not type.

Raglan sleeve

Set-in sleeve

My personal brand favorite is Jerzees, which I have found to live up to its reputation for being pill-free. This is especially important if you have spent time and effort embellishing a project, such as a sweatshirt dress (page 46), only to find that after two washings, little balls have formed all over the fabric. Not only is it very discouraging, but the little balls are virtually impossible to remove. (I have tried everything from tape to razor blades!) Jerzees brand is widely available at a favorable price, especially at major discount stores.

A word about sizing: When I specify a men's sweatshirt in the materials list, inquiring minds will want to know why! For my Quik-Quilt™ technique, I will be showing you how to machine quilt onto the actual sweatshirt. Because you will be taking the sweatshirt apart and stitching all over it, the sweatshirt needs to a have a looser fit than you might normally prefer to wear. Remember also that sweatshirts are stretchy, and when you remove that stretch, you must add some ease for comfort. You can do that by purchasing a man's sweatshirt that is slightly baggy on you. I have noticed lately that sweatshirt sizing seems to be growing roomier (does that mean that our men are watching even more football and wrestling?) so try on each sweatshirt to check for fit before you start your project. While you can alter the jacket or dress if it is too big, why not avoid that task by checking the fit first?

PREWASHING SWEATSHIRTS

Since you will surely be laundering the finished garment in the future, it's always a good idea to follow the manufacturer's guidelines, and to prewash and preshrink purchased sweatshirts (and all fabrics you intend to use) before the garment is cut and assembled. I still live by the doctrine of Miss Irma Walters, my home economics teacher, who advised: "Better to be safe than sorry!"

PREPARING THE SWEATSHIRT FOR EMBELLISHMENT, QUILTING, AND FINISHING

1. Prepare the sweatshirt by removing the neck and bottom ribbing. Simply cut it away, using a rotary cutter and ruler to even the bottom raw edge if necessary. (*Do not* spend time struggling with a seam ripper, or you'll never get to sew!)

2. Remove the sleeves in the same fashion. If the project calls for a quilted sleeve, remove the cuffs and the underarm seams as well.

Sweatshirt with neck
and bottom ribbing
and sleeves removed

Sleeve open
with underarm seam
and ribbed cuff removed

3. Cut away the shoulder seams. (You are left with a shell of a sweatshirt that looks like a football team has been at it!) Smooth the shirt on your worktable, and carefully cut away the front at the side seams. Trim off the side seams.

4. Fold the front of the shirt in half to find the center point. Crease or mark the center point—top and bottom—with pins. Use a long ruler or yardstick to draw a line down the center, from the neck to the bottom edge of the shirt front. Using scissors or a rotary cutter, cut directly on the center line. You now have 2 front halves and a back unit for your project. The specific project instructions will take you from here.

Sweatshirt front

Front cut at center line

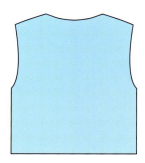

Sweatshirt back

Basic Construction Information

Grain Line: When laying out the commercial pattern pieces for your project, please note any grain lines marked on the tissue. Your finished garment will look nicer if you do. Note that each of my pattern pieces is also marked with a grain-line arrow if applicable.

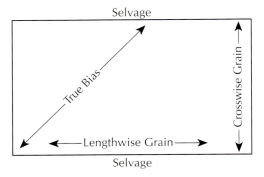

Seam Allowances: Unless otherwise specified, my techniques and instructions use ¼"-wide seam allowances. When working with a commercial pattern to construct the base garment, please follow the pattern guidelines.

RST: This is my shorthand for "right sides together." I won't bore you with the details!

Chain Piecing: This efficient machine-piecing technique is ideal for sewing identical multiple units. Pair the pieces, RST, with the same fabric piece always on top. Stack the pairs near your machine so that the edge to be stitched faces to the right (for example, toward the presser foot). Feed the first pair under the presser foot, stitching a ¼"-wide seam as usual. Do not end with a backstitch and do not clip the thread. Instead, take a few stitches, then carefully feed the next pair under the presser foot. A chain of thread will connect the sewn units. Continue sewing until all of the pairs are stitched, then clip the connecting threads. Press as usual.

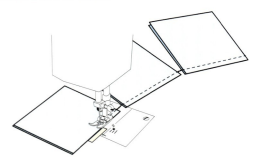

Ripping a seam is never fun. Ripping a whole *chain* of seams is a nightmare! Chain piecing saves time—if you work carefully. Be sure that the first pair is sewn correctly before proceeding.

Clean Finishing/Serging: This is just a fancy way of telling you to do something to the edges of your fabric so they won't ravel and look ugly when someone looks at the inside of your garment! Seriously though, at certain times finishing is truly necessary, and the instructions will indicate when. If you have a serger, you know that one pass through the machine is all you need to cut and overcast the offending seam. If you don't have a serger, put it on your wish list. In the meantime, you can use pinking shears (yikes!) or, better yet, check your machine to see if it offers a suitable overcast stitch. (Sometimes we forget what our machines are capable of, so check your manual.) If all else fails, a small zigzag stitch run down the edges of each seam will do the trick.

When you determine the correct settings for your zigzag overcast, note it for future reference and keep it near your machine.

Hems: To hem simple dresses made from flannel or cotton, straighten any raw edges, turn the raw edge under a generous ¼" and press well. Use an adjustable 6" ruler set to 2" and turn up the hem to that measurement. Pin as you go and press. Take the garment to the machine and stitch around close to the ¼" folded edge. Remember: your top thread will be sewn to the underside of your garment, so be sure to check your *bobbin* for the appropriate-color thread.

If you prefer, hems may be stitched by hand.

USING THE APPLIQUÉ PATTERNS

The machine-appliqué technique used in this book does not require turning seam allowances. Instead, fused fabric is used for most of the appliqués. Fusible web gives a clean, sharp edge to the shapes and eliminates the time-consuming step of turning under seam allowances. That's what makes it so quick and easy!

There are many good ways to machine appliqué, and if you already have a favorite method that works well for you, stick with it. But for those who want to know how I do it, the following should provide some direction.

Since the appliqué pattern pieces are bound into this book, you will probably want to copy the pages you need for the project. (Depending upon the size of the intended wearer, you may need to adjust the size of some of the appliqué shapes a bit to arrange them just like those in the project photos.) If you don't have access to a copy machine, you may trace the designs onto template plastic. This sturdy plastic is available in sheets at most quilt stores. Please be sure to note on each template what it is, how many to cut, and whether the cuts will be regular or reverse. The latter makes a difference in some projects, such as the mittens on page 27, because you don't want your thumbs all pointing west! It also saves confusion when you are busily arranging the appliqués onto the garment.

Once you have your templates marked and cut, you are ready to trace the shapes onto the fused (or unfused) fabric. For a *regular* appliqué piece, place the appliqué template with the writing *face down* onto the paper side of fused fabric or the wrong side of unfused fabric. With unfused fabric such as craft felt that doesn't have a wrong or right side, just pick a side and trace. To trace, I use a .05 lead mechanical pencil. If that doesn't show on a dark fabric, I have been known to use just about anything that will give me a line. There, I have, 'fessed up!

When you need to trace a *reversed* appliqué piece, place the template *face up* on the paper side of the fused fabric or the wrong side of the unfused fabric to get the desired orientation.

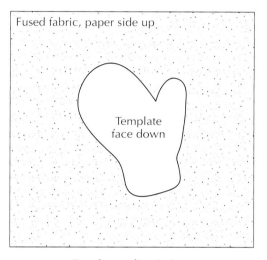

Regular appliqué piece

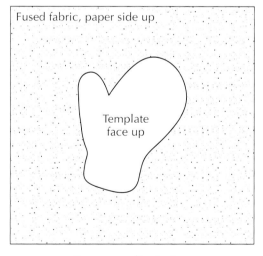

Reverse appliqué piece

WORKING WITH FUSIBLES

I add a rather unorthodox, but timesaving step to my fusing procedure, which I'll share here with you. If you prefer the more traditional methods, refer to the manufacturer's guidelines, usually found on the end of the bolt or right on the packaging.

I like to keep fused scraps of different colors and prints on hand for future use, so anytime I am working on a project with new fabric, I cut a larger-than-necessary, equally sized square of both the fabric and the fusible. This square might measure 6" x 6" or 12" x 12", depending on my mood or how much fabric I have.

After I've used my iron to bond the fabric and fusible together, I take the fused fabric (with paper still intact) to my worktable and trace my templates. Then I cut out the appliqués I need, and put the remaining fused fabric into a bin. Whenever a future project calls for fused fabric, I can go to my bin, make a selection, trace, and cut.

There are many brands and varieties of fusible webbing available—something for every seamstress and crafter, and for every type of project. It is important that you choose the correct type for machine sewing, or you will end up frustrated by skipped stitches and gummy needles. If the product information leaves you uncertain, be sure to ask your quilt-shop staff. They will guide you to the correct product.

CONSTRUCTING LOG CABIN BLOCKS

Building a Log Cabin block is easy. The instructions for each garment will tell you how many different strips to cut and how wide to cut them. The instructions will also tell you how many center squares to cut and how large to cut them.

To assemble a Log Cabin block, place the center square and a randomly chosen fabric strip RST. Sew the strip to the square, taking the usual ¼"-wide seam allowance. Open, press the seam away from the center square, and trim the strip even with the edge of the center square.

Continue to add randomly selected strips, proceeding around the center square in a clockwise direction. Press and trim each strip before adding the next one. Continue adding strips in this fashion until the block reaches the required size.

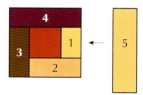

MAKING AND ATTACHING BINDING

I never do the "B" word (bias). When my design calls for binding, cut a strip or several strips of fabric as directed, usually 1½" wide. Cut the strips on the straight of grain, either lengthwise or crosswise—whichever gives you the longest strip. The gentle curves of these garments can be perfectly bound without the hassle of making bias strips.

After the strips have been cut, join them with a ¼"-wide seam on their short ends to make one long strip. For adult garments, three joined strips are usually sufficient. For children's garments, I use two so that I won't run short. I hate to add when I am in the middle of sewing on the binding!

After your strips are joined and the seams pressed open, you are ready to pin-baste the binding to the garment. Pin the binding RST with the garment, raw edges even. Choose an inconspicuious spot to start. Fold the beginning (short end) of the binding over ½" to create a finished edge. Pin-baste the binding around the entire garment, using extra pins to work in any fullness around curves. Overlap the remaining binding over the starting fold, and trim any excess. Stitch, using a ¼"-wide seam allowance. Clip any curves, and press the binding gently toward the back, covering the raw edges. On the inside of the garment, turn the binding under ¼" and pin-baste to just cover the seam line. Use a hand blind stitch to sew the binding to the garment.

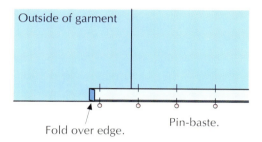

Outside of garment

Fold over edge. Pin-baste.

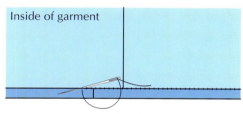

Inside of garment

Turn to inside of garment, turn raw edge, and stitch.

When binding an armhole, start at the underarm point so the starting and ending seam is invisible.

Embellishing Techniques

BRAIDING

A braid is a braid . . . is a braid! The technique is exactly what you'd expect it to be: three strands of fiber interwoven to form a single, stronger decorative length. In layman's terms, it's like braiding one's hair. That's all there is to it. I do have a few tips, though.

First, assemble the strips of whatever fibers you're using and bundle them together, keeping the top edges even. Make a quick machine stitch straight across the top edge of the bundle to secure it. Pin the stitched section to the edge of the ironing board. (It's easier to braid if the bundle is secured to the edge of something stable.) After you have finished braiding the entire length, secure the remaining ends with a pin before unfastening the braid from the ironing board. Go back to the machine and stitch across the finishing end to secure. That really is all there is to it!

I like to braid different types of fabrics and fibers (such as twine) for flowers and fasteners. We will be doing some of this later. I am sure that once you try it, you will be writing me with creative new ways to use this technique.

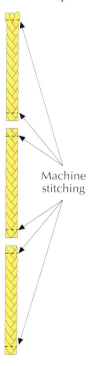

Machine stitching

When project instructions call for making flowers, you will be asked to measure, cut, and stitch certain lengths. You must remember to stitch across the finishing end of each segment before cutting to keep the braid from unraveling.

Note: Some projects require that you cut two identical pieces of one fiber, such as twine, then two equal lengths of a second fiber (see "Fleece 'n Flannel Jackets" on page 75). One fiber pair acts as a single "strand," so you'll still have the three necessary strands. The resulting braid has more texture and pizzazz.

DECORATIVE STITCHES

These are the fancy (that is, non-straight) stitches on your machine that the dealer raved about, but you've never used! My personal favorites are the feather and blanket stitch. Don't be afraid to experiment. Even if you consider your machine too dated to do anything fancy, double-check your user's guide. You may be pleasantly surprised. If not, play around with the zigzag stitch. A little width here, a little length there, and you'll soon have a nice decorative stitch to use.

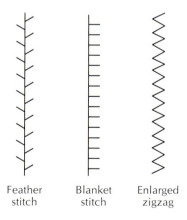

Feather stitch   Blanket stitch   Enlarged zigzag

Thread your sewing-machine needle with two spools of the same color thread when doing decorative stitching. This gives a denser, hand-done look to your stitching. I can keep a secret if you can!

KNOTTED LEAVES

The garments on pages 34–35 are embellished with darling (if I do say so myself) knotted felt leaves. (I know it doesn't sound humble, but I *did* think them up.) They are so simple to make.

To make one, trace the leaf template onto *unfused* craft felt and cut out. Grab the ends of each leaf and tie in a knot. (You know, the first step in tying your shoe.) That's it, that's the secret formula. Don't tie it too tightly though, or the knot will be too puny. Straighten out the leaf ends, and you are ready to attach the leaf to whatever you are embellishing.

PRAIRIE STITCH

This is my name for a big, primitive running stitch made by hand. For the best results, use the "full strength" (all strands) of your favorite embroidery floss. This is a no-fuss, no-muss technique. Don't worry if your stitches are not the same length. The operative word here is "primitive," not haute couture. I like to use a chenille needle in the 18–22 size range. It has a big eye for my poor eyes! Knot one end of the floss and, beginning from the underside to hide the knot, make stitches approximately ½" long. Don't labor over the stitches; just *stitch* them and you'll get the best look. When you get to the end of a section or need to add more floss, simply tie off with a knot on the underside and begin again.

SQUIGGLE AND STITCH

Sounds technical, doesn't it? It's not. There isn't a right or wrong way to do this technique. When the instructions call for a "squiggle and stitch," just follow the illustration below to "squiggle" the base fiber, and secure with a zigzag stitch. You can have as many squiggles as you desire.

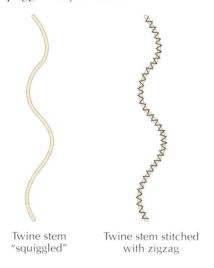

Twine stem   Twine stem stitched
"squiggled"   with zigzag

YO-YOS

These little babies are so versatile! As you'll see throughout this book, they make terrific flowers and can embellish just about anything. Mine is not the traditional method, but a speedy technique that works well for embellishment purposes.

1. Use your preferred template material to trace and cut the circle template given with the pattern.

2. Thread a needle with a double length of regular sewing thread. Knot the ends.

3. Make a regular-sized running stitch a scant ¼" from the edge, all around the circle. Don't knot, but gently pull the thread and gather the circle into a little pouch with the right side facing out. Use your fingers to flatten, smooth, and center the bunched fabric.

4. Take a few stitches through the center of the yo-yo and tie off on the wrong side. Cut the thread and—voilà!—you've made a yo-yo!

Machine-Quilting Techniques

FREE-MOTION QUILTING

This machine-quilting technique is so much fun! What a treat to create quilted fabric in any color or print that you want, without relying on what is commercially available.

Follow these instructions when a project calls for free-motion quilting:

1. Thread the machine with a color of your choice. Be certain that the bobbin is full.

2. Change the presser foot to the darning foot (see "Special Machine Attachments" on page 9).

3. Drop the machine's feed dogs. These are the metal teeth that move your fabric under the presser foot. Refer to your machine's manual if you are rusty at doing this.

For a neat, professional-looking finish, match the bobbin thread to the inside color of the garment.

4. Set the stitch length for a smidgen higher than the normal setting. On my machine, the normal setting is 2, so I set it at 2½. Choose a corner or other comfortable area to begin stitching. Pull the bobbin thread through to the top, and stitch by gently guiding the fabric under the needle in loops and squiggles. You'll probably need to practice a little to get a feel for this. (Take a deep breath and relax; you cannot make a mistake!) You'll soon feel a rhythm developing. You can stop and reposition your hands at anytime. That's all there is to it! There are hoops you can use with this technique, and some of my students swear by them. I prefer to just use my hands, but I encourage you to try different methods until you find one you like.

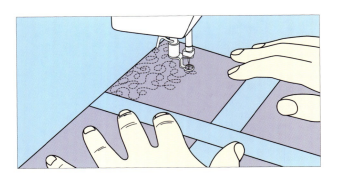

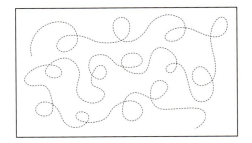

CROSSHATCH QUILTING

This is another version of machine quilting that I often use with great results.

1. Use a long ruler or yardstick and chalk or disappearing marker to draw a diagonal line from one shoulder tip of the cut-up garment to its opposite bottom corner. This will be your guide for marking subsequent quilting lines.

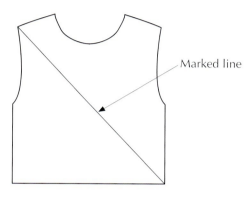

Marked line

2. Use your see-through ruler to mark additional, parallel quilting lines at 1" intervals. Mark all lines for one direction first, then mark the lines in the opposite direction to form a grid.

3. Take the garment to your sewing machine, choose a comfortable area to begin, and quilt along the premarked lines. You don't need to drop the machine's feed dogs for this straight-line stitching. A walking foot attachment helps keep the layers from shifting as you stitch, but it is not essential (see "Special Machine Attachments" on page 9).

Begin here . . .   . . . and here.

SHAGGY PLUSH JACKETS

Shaggy plush felt reminds me of a cuddly stuffed animal, and that memory is exactly what got me started using this great fabric for clothing. I kept seeing wonderful soft bunnies and bears made up in shaggy plush at the various trade shows and conventions I attended. The fabric was so fluffy I just couldn't keep my hands off! I started dreaming of ways to use it in apparel, and soon after, developed my first-ever garment from shaggy plush felt, which I named "The Thready Bare Jacket."

Naturally, I wanted opinions from those around me, to see if they shared my enthusiasm for this new fiber and design. I excitedly showed my friend Jensey, whose taste I greatly admire. She looked at me and said, "That looks like a hairy back!" before she started giggling. Undaunted, I continued with the "Great Shaggy Plush Experiment," and the rest—as they say—is history! That particular jacket went on to be Threadbare's all-time bestseller, and paved the way for more shaggy felt creations, including the two new designs you'll find here. It just goes to show what thinking "off the bolt" can do! By the way, Jensey is still my friend—and now sports several garments made from shaggy plush felt!

WINTER BLESSINGS: ADULT JACKET

MATERIALS: 42"-WIDE FABRIC

A favorite lined jacket pattern with round collar and no cuffs

Shaggy plush felt for the jacket*

Coordinating lining fabric for jacket*

¼ yd. of coordinating checked fabric, preferably cotton or homespun, for scallop appliqués

¼ yd. of washable felt for collar inset and mitten appliqués

Craft-size squares (9" x 12") or ⅛-yd. pieces of washable felt in 4 assorted colors for winter appliqués

2 yds. of fusible web

¼ yd. of Warm & Natural batting

Assorted skeins of coordinating embroidery floss

14 wooden buttons, ½" diameter

*Refer to the pattern packaging for the specific yardage in your size.

Look for a loose-fitting jacket pattern with lining, no fussy details, and a simple collar style. I prefer the rounded collar, but another style could work just as well. Choosing one without cuffs will keep you from fiddling with the sleeves, trying to adapt the pattern. If you love pockets in your outerwear, choose a pattern with side pockets. Patch pockets on the front would interfere with the appliqué designs.

Note: Refer to "Techniques, Terminology, and Tips" on pages 6–19 for guidance in preparing and assembling this garment.

CUTTING OUT THE JACKET

Prewash the shaggy plush felt and lining fabric (see the tips for shaggy plush felt on page 7). Using the pattern pieces from the jacket pattern, cut the jacket fronts, back, and sleeves from the shaggy plush and lining fabrics.

PREPARING, FUSING, AND EMBELLISHING THE COLLAR

1. Prepare the washable felt and other fabrics for fusing (see "Fusible Web" on page 8 and "Working with Fusibles" on page 14.)

2. You will be using only the front part of the collar. Depending on your pattern, the collar piece may be too large and may need some adjustment. Lay the collar pattern on the jacket front as shown, allowing for the center front seam allowance. Mark and trim any excess collar tissue at the shoulder line, allowing for the shoulder seam allowance. Cut a right and left collar from the fused washable felt.

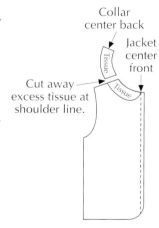

Collar center back
Jacket center front
Cut away excess tissue at shoulder line.

3. Lay each washable felt collar piece face up on the right side (fluffy side) of the batting. Leave at least 1" between the pieces. Fuse the collar pieces to the batting. Cut out each collar piece, leaving a generous ¼" of batting around the outside edge. Trim batting at the neckline edge even with the collar.

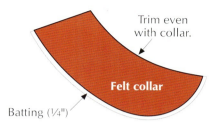

Trim even with collar.
Felt collar
Batting (¼")

4. Sew a decorative stitch, such as a feather stitch, around the edge of the felt as shown (see "Decorative Stitches" on page 16).

5. Using the pattern on page 32, make a collar holly leaf template. Trace and cut out 4 holly leaf appliqués from the fused washable felt (see "Using the Appliqué Patterns" on page 13). Fuse the leaves to the collar as shown, and stitch around each leaf with a decorative stitch.

6. Finish each collar piece around the outside edge with a prairie stitch as shown (see "Prairie Stitch" on page 16).

COLLAR DETAIL

Preparing and Fusing the Jacket Appliqués

1. Cut a 6" x 24" piece of checked cotton or homespun fabric and bond it to the fusible web. Using the pattern on page 32, make a scallop template. Trace and cut 3 sections of scallop, each 24" long, from the fused fabric, using the template as a guide to get you started. (If you prefer, you may cut the scallops freehand.) Cut additional lengths as needed.

2. Using the photo on page 22 as a guide, cut and arrange the fused scallop strips across the right front panel of the jacket. (Remember: you are looking at a photo, so the right front panel is actually on the left in the photo!) Don't worry if your scallops don't look exactly like the photo. Remember, it's creativity that counts! Fuse each strip in place and stitch around each with a decorative stitch. I used my machine blanket stitch.

3. Make templates for the jacket appliqués using the pattern pieces on pages 32–33. Notice that some patterns are for both the adult and child jackets, some are for the adult jacket only, and others are for the child jacket only. Bond washable felt to the fusible web, then trace and cut out the "adult" appliqués.

4. Arrange and fuse the appropriate appliqués to the right front jacket panel. Stay within the scallop sections as shown in the photo on page 22. Fuse 1 each of the regular and reverse mittens and mitten hearts, the tree, star, wreath, bow, snowman, scarf (both pieces), bird and wing, and stocking with heel and toe reinforcements; 2 each of the mitten cuffs; and 3 of the holly leaves.

5. Use a decorative stitch to stitch around each appliqué. I used a machine blanket stitch.

6. Add embroidery touches to each appliqué as desired. Try little cross-stitches for the wreath, and a chain stitch for the tree garland, carrot, and stick limbs on the snowman. Let your imagination be your guide.

7. Repeat step 1 to cut 3 scallop strips. Arrange, fuse, and decorate the scallop strips on the left front jacket panel as shown in the detail photo. Be sure to leave room for the words "Winter Blessings." When you are satisfied with the placement, fuse and stitch around each as before.

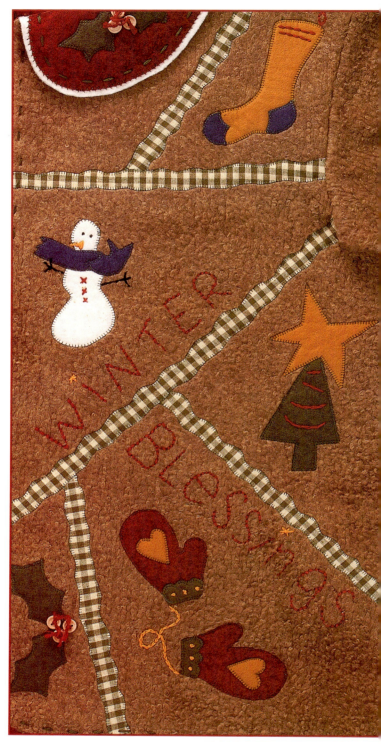

DETAIL: LEFT FRONT JACKET PANEL

8. Refer to the detail photo on page 24 for placement, then mark and embroider the words "Winter Blessings" in a primitive backstitch. Place, fuse, and stitch the following fused appliqués: 1 each of the regular and reverse mittens and mitten hearts, reverse stocking, reverse heel and toe reinforcements, tree, star, reverse snowman, and reverse scarf (both pieces); and 2 each of the holly leaves and mitten cuffs. Embellish as desired.

9. Center the remaining 2 mittens, cuffs, and mitten hearts on the back of the jacket, approximately 4½" down from the collar line as shown. Fuse and stitch them in place; embellish with embroidery as desired.

JACKET BACK DETAIL

CUTTING, FUSING, AND ASSEMBLING THE SLEEVES

1. Make a template using the sleeve heart pattern on page 33. Bond a piece of washable felt to fusible web, then cut out 2 heart pieces. Fuse each heart to a piece of batting; cut and stitch as for the collar pieces (see "Preparing, Fusing, and Embellishing the Collar" on page 23).

Note: Leave ¼" of batting all around the outside edge of each heart.

2. Prepare 2 additional scallop strips (see "Preparing and Fusing the Jacket Appliqués" on page 24). Mark each sleeve 2½" up from its hemline, then position and fuse 1 scallop strip around each sleeve at the mark, as shown in the photo. Finish the scallops with decorative stitching as before.

SLEEVE DETAIL

3. Position a heart with batting in the center of each sleeve, angled slightly over the scallop. Fuse and finish with decorative stitching.

ASSEMBLING AND FINISHING THE JACKET

1. Pin-baste the fused collar pieces to each front jacket panel, keeping in mind the center front seam allowances dictated by your pattern. Follow the pattern instructions to assemble the jacket and add the lining. Press the jacket well on the lining side. I like to use starch here to get a crisp finish. If you prefer, you can press with steam.

Front centers

Seam allowance

C reate wonderful gift containers for all occasions by fusing any of the appliqués featured in this book onto brown bags or box lids.

2. To complete this jacket in style (and keep the lining from rolling out!), finish with a prairie stitch all around the jacket edge. Start at the bottom side-seam area and stitch approximately ½" from the finished edge.

Prairie stitch

3. Use embroidery floss to sew 3 wooden buttons in the center of each holly bouquet, and 1 button in the center of each sleeve heart.

Companion Project : Quik Winter Mittens

3. Bond felt scraps to fusible web and cut out a few holiday shapes. You can use the ones from the jacket pattern if you like or draw your own. Fuse and stitch the appliqués to the right sides of the mitten shapes.

4. "Free-hand" cut and fuse a scallop cuff to each mitten.

5. For each mitten, cut a piece of flannel and 2 pieces of batting. Cut the pieces at least 3" larger than the mitten shape all around. Stack them as follows: flannel face down, 1 piece of batting face (fluffy side) down, second piece of batting face up, and finally the mitten shape face up, in the middle of the stack. Pin-baste the layers.

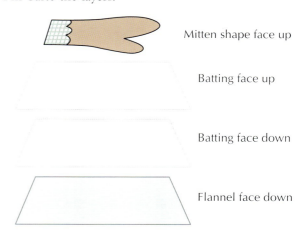

Mitten shape face up

Batting face up

Batting face down

Flannel face down

Here's a quick and fun idea to use up shaggy plush felt, fleece, flannel, and washable felt fabric scraps! All you need is some fusible web and batting.

1. Use a favorite mitten pattern or draw a generous template of your own hand. (If drawing your own, be sure to widen the wrist so you can get the mittens on. Otherwise, you'll have a set of winter-style potholders!)

2. Trace the mitten template on the wrong side of the shaggy plush felt or fleece fabric. Don't forget to turn the template face up for one mitten, and face down (or reverse) for the other. Cut out the mitten shapes.

Wrong side of fabric

Wrong side of fabric

6. Use your sewing machine to sew a decorative stitch around the perimeter of the mitten, leaving the cuff area free. Carefully trim away the excess fabric, leaving a generous ¼" of batting and flannel showing. Complete the cuff with embroidery.

WINTER WISHES: CHILD'S JACKET

MATERIALS: 42"-WIDE FABRIC

A favorite lined jacket pattern with round collar and no cuffs

Shaggy plush felt for the jacket*

Coordinating lining fabric for the jacket*

1/8 yd. of coordinating checked fabric, preferably cotton or homespun, for scallop appliqués

1/8 yd. of washable felt for collar inset

Craft-size squares (9" x 12") or 1/8-yd. pieces of washable felt in 4 assorted colors for winter appliqués

1 yd. of fusible web

1/8 yd. of Warm & Natural batting

Assorted skeins of coordinating embroidery floss

5 wooden buttons, 1/2" diameter

*Refer to the pattern packaging for the specific yardage in your child's size.

Note: Refer to "Techniques, Terminology, and Tips" on pages 6–19 for guidance in preparing and assembling this garment.

CUTTING THE JACKET AND PREPARING THE COLLAR

Follow the instructions for "Winter Blessings" to cut the jacket and assemble the collar (see "Cutting Out the Jacket" and "Preparing, Fusing, and Embellishing the Collar" on page 23). Use the same collar holly-leaf pattern on page 32 to make the template and cut the 4 collar holly leaf appliqués.

PREPARING AND FUSING THE JACKET APPLIQUÉS

1. Follow the instructions for "Winter Blessings" to cut and fuse 2 scallop strips from the checked fabric. (You may need to cut more, depending on the child's size.) Work with 4" x 24" pieces of checked fabric (see "Preparing and Fusing the Jacket Appliqués" on page 24). Position, fuse, and stitch the scallops on the front panels as described. Use the photo on page 28 as a placement guide.

2. Follow step 3 of the adult instructions on page 24 to fuse, trace, and cut the appliqués. Use the child patterns on pages 31–33 to make the templates and to cut the appropriate number of appliqués.

3. Referring to the photo, position, fuse, and stitch the following appliqués to the right front jacket panel: 1 regular and 1 reverse of the candy cane; 1 each of the mitten, mitten cuff, mitten heart, stocking with heel and toe reinforcements, snowman face, snowman hat, snowman-hat holly, and scarf (both pieces).

4. Complete the left front jacket panel by embroidering the words "Winter Wishes" in a primitive backstitch as shown in the detail photo. Place, fuse, and stitch the following appliqués: 1 each of the regular and reverse skates, skate cuffs, and skate blades, the bow, gift box, gift box ribbon, and star.

5. Add embroidery to each appliqué as desired. Try little cross-stitches for trim on the stocking, big cross-stitches for laces on the skates, and "coal and carrot" embellishments on the snowman face. Get creative with that embroidery floss!

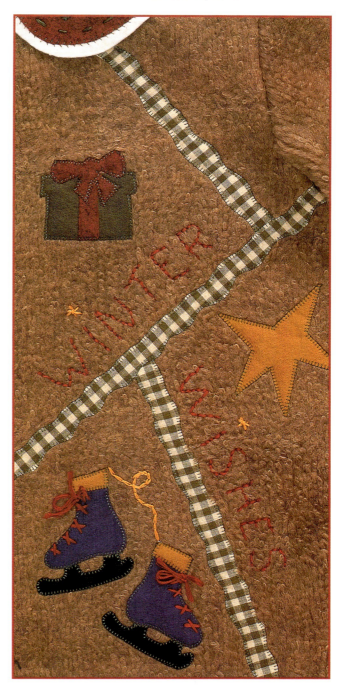

DETAIL: LEFT FRONT JACKET PANEL

6. Center the remaining left and right skates and skate blades, and the 2 skate cuffs on the back of the jacket, approximately 4" down from the neckline as shown. Fuse and stitch them in place, then embellish with embroidery as desired.

JACKET BACK DETAIL

CUTTING, FUSING, AND ASSEMBLING THE SLEEVES

Make a template using the sleeve heart pattern on page 33. Follow the instructions for the adult jacket on page 25 to cut and prepare 2 additional scallop strips and 2 hearts with batting. Mark the sleeves as described in the adult instructions. Position, fuse, and embroider the sleeve appliqués.

SLEEVE DETAIL

ASSEMBLING AND FINISHING THE JACKET

Refer to the instructions for "Winter Blessings" to pin-baste and attach the fused collar pieces to each front jacket panel (see "Assembling and Finishing the Jacket" on page 26). Use the prairie stitch to finish the jacket's edge, and embroidery floss to add 1 wooden button to each holly bouquet, 1 to each sleeve heart, and 1 to the snowman's hat.

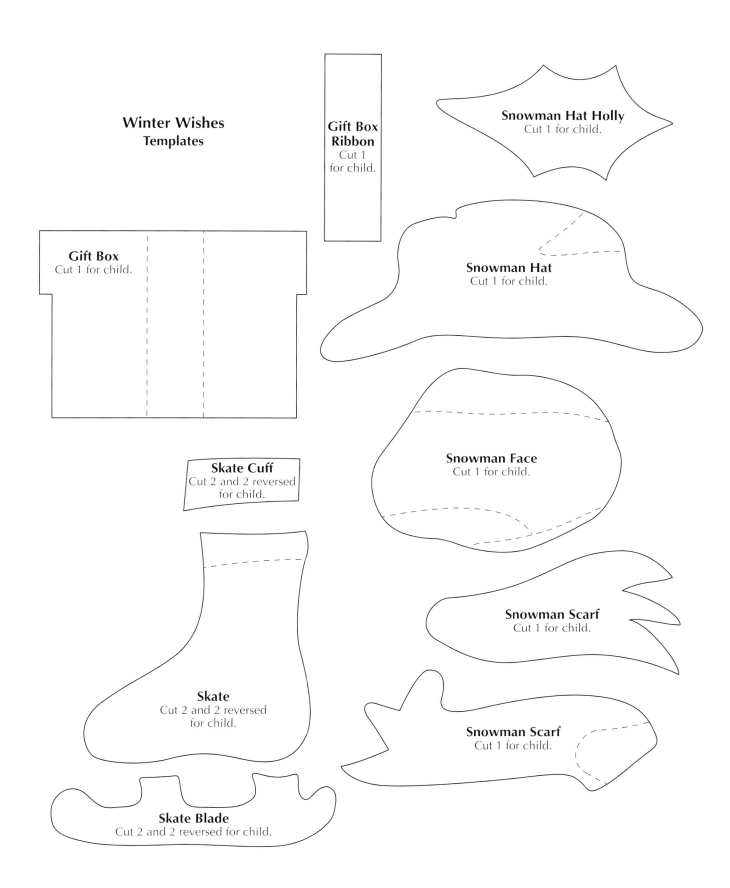

Winter Wishes
Templates

Gift Box Ribbon
Cut 1 for child.

Snowman Hat Holly
Cut 1 for child.

Gift Box
Cut 1 for child.

Snowman Hat
Cut 1 for child.

Skate Cuff
Cut 2 and 2 reversed for child.

Snowman Face
Cut 1 for child.

Snowman Scarf
Cut 1 for child.

Skate
Cut 2 and 2 reversed for child.

Snowman Scarf
Cut 1 for child.

Skate Blade
Cut 2 and 2 reversed for child.

Winter Blessings / Winter Wishes
Templates

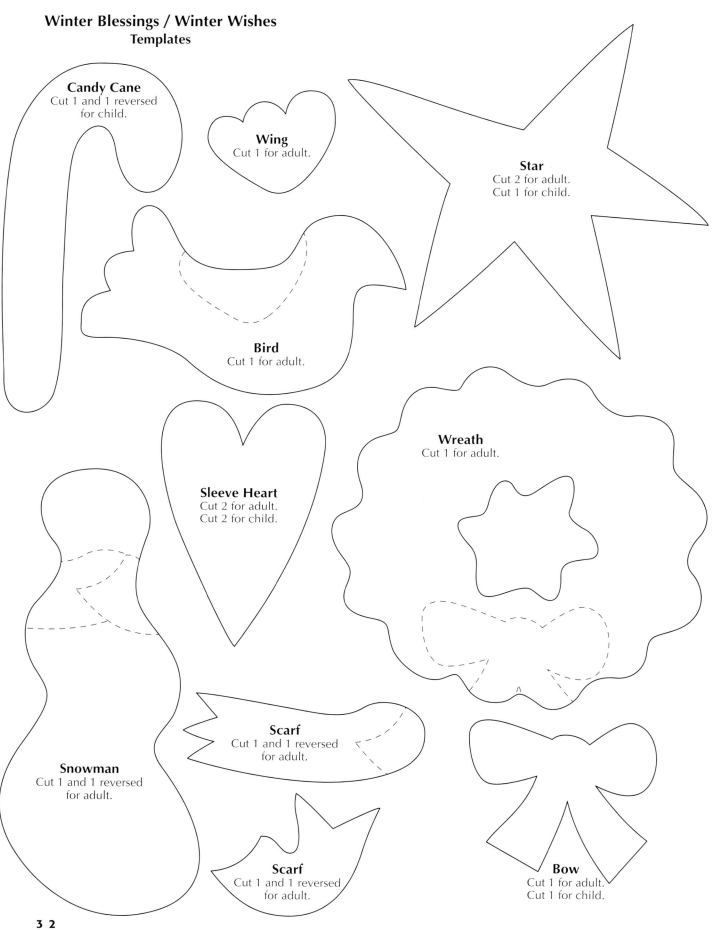

Candy Cane
Cut 1 and 1 reversed
for child.

Wing
Cut 1 for adult.

Star
Cut 2 for adult.
Cut 1 for child.

Bird
Cut 1 for adult.

Sleeve Heart
Cut 2 for adult.
Cut 2 for child.

Wreath
Cut 1 for adult.

Snowman
Cut 1 and 1 reversed
for adult.

Scarf
Cut 1 and 1 reversed
for adult.

Scarf
Cut 1 and 1 reversed
for adult.

Bow
Cut 1 for adult.
Cut 1 for child.

Winter Blessings / Winter Wishes
Templates

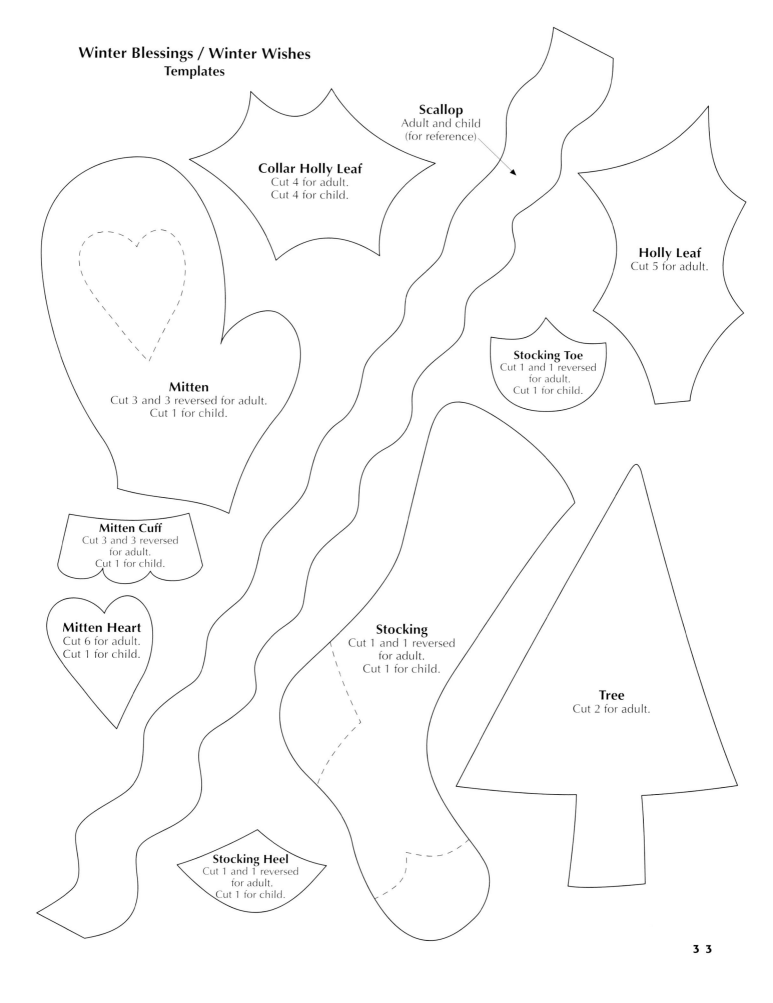

Collar Holly Leaf
Cut 4 for adult.
Cut 4 for child.

Scallop
Adult and child
(for reference)

Holly Leaf
Cut 5 for adult.

Stocking Toe
Cut 1 and 1 reversed
for adult.
Cut 1 for child.

Mitten
Cut 3 and 3 reversed for adult.
Cut 1 for child.

Mitten Cuff
Cut 3 and 3 reversed
for adult.
Cut 1 for child.

Mitten Heart
Cut 6 for adult.
Cut 1 for child.

Stocking
Cut 1 and 1 reversed
for adult.
Cut 1 for child.

Tree
Cut 2 for adult.

Stocking Heel
Cut 1 and 1 reversed
for adult.
Cut 1 for child.

PLUSH AND FLANNEL OVERALLS

Overalls are just plain fun to wear, and these plush and flannel overalls are fun to make, too. I'll get you started with the plush felt bodice, Log Cabin patches, and yo-yo flower embellishments, but don't stop there! Add your own personal touches to make them even more special. Think what you could do with Log Cabin patch pockets, or a yo-yo flower and twine stem winding down the leg. You'll have fun collecting the compliments when you wear these.

Just a reminder: shaggy plush felt and plush felt have two distinct looks. Keep that in mind when selecting the fabric for this project.

COUNTRY CHIC: ADULT OVERALLS

MATERIALS: 42"-WIDE FABRIC

A favorite overalls pattern

Plush felt for bib section of overalls*

Print flannel for trouser section of overalls*

Contrasting flannel for bib lining, straps, and pockets*

13 pieces (⅛ yd. each) or assorted flannel scraps (totaling 1⅝ yds.) in coordinating colors for Log Cabin blocks and yo-yos

1 craft-size square of dark green washable felt (9" x 12") for leaves

½ yd. of fusible web

2 pieces of jute twine, each 36" long

Assorted skeins of embroidery floss

4 porcelain flower buttons**

*Refer to the pattern packaging for the specific yardage in your size.

**See "Resources" on page 95. You may need additional "plain" buttons if your pattern requires them for side closures.

When choosing an overalls pattern, look for simple styling, such as a plain bib and easy-to-insert pockets. Don't be shy about (carefully!) opening the pattern and checking the instructions for any construction detail that you aren't confident about, before making your decision. But please return the instructions to the pattern pack in the correct order. Your thoughtfulness will be appreciated by the next stitcher.

Since overalls are usually donned with the aid of some sort of side fastening, be sure that your machine buttonholer is in working order, or that you are confident working with heavy-duty snaps.

Note: Refer to "Techniques, Terminology, and Tips" on pages 6–19 for guidance in preparing and assembling this garment.

Cutting Out the Overalls

Using the pattern pieces for the overalls, cut the pieces for the bib section from the plush felt, the trousers from the print flannel, and the bib lining, straps, and pockets from the contrasting flannel. Set these pieces aside.

Making the Log Cabin Blocks

1. Now for the fun! Begin by deciding which one of your flannel scraps (or ⅛-yard pieces) will be the center square for your Log Cabin blocks. Cut three 2½" squares from that fabric.

2. From your remaining flannel scraps (or ⅛-yard pieces), cut 1½"-wide strips of 12 different colors and prints. Cut the fabric so that you get the longest strips possible.

3. Assemble 3 Log Cabin blocks, using the 2½" squares for the centers and adding the 1½"-wide strips for the logs. Prints and colors may be chosen randomly, but proceed around the center block in the order indicated by the illustration (see "Constructing Log Cabin Blocks" on page 14). Make 2

blocks measuring 6½" x 6½", including the seam allowance, and 1 block measuring 8½" x 8½".

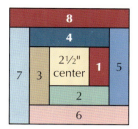

Make 2.

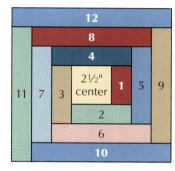

Make 1.

4. Back each block with fusible web (see "Fusible Web" on page 8) and square up the block if necessary. Cut 1 of the 6½" blocks in half on the diagonal—don't be nervous!—and 1 block in half crosswise. Remove the paper backing from all of the cut pieces. Lay the front bib section face up on the worktable. Arrange the triangles and rectangles across the bottom edge of the bib section, either as shown in the detail, or as desired. You'll leave the 8½" Log Cabin block intact.

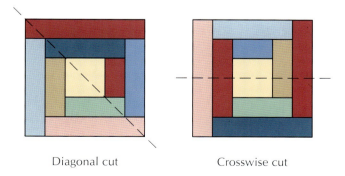

Diagonal cut   Crosswise cut

5. Fuse the "fractured" Log Cabin blocks in place, then stitch around each triangle and square with a prairie stitch or another decorative stitch (see "Prairie Stitch" on page 16). Trim any excess Log Cabin block from the bottom and side edges of the bib. Don't worry about decorative stitching on these edges. They will be hidden by the seam allowance when the overalls are stitched together.

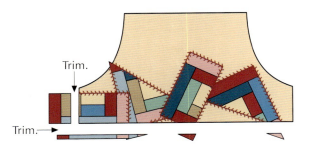

Here's a neat tip for a cute—and quick—gift! Make a large yo-yo by starting with a luncheon plate–sized circle. Then embellish the yo-yo with braid flowers, porcelain buttons, or knotted felt leaves. Hand stitch or hot-glue a pin clasp to the back of the yo-yo for a whimsical brooch. Your friends will love you for it!

MAKING THE FLOWER, STEM, AND LEAF EMBELLISHMENTS

1. Make a template using the yo-yo circle pattern on page 43. Make 2 yo-yos from leftover flannel (see "Yo-Yos" on page 17).

2. Cut 1 piece of jute twine 9" long, another 7" long, and a third 4" long. Squiggle and pin the twine stems down the front of the bib. Refer to the bib front detail on page 37 as necessary. Stitch over each stem with a wide zigzag stitch (see "Squiggle and Stitch" on page 17).

3. Place a yo-yo at the top of 2 stems and tack in place. Sew a flower button in the center of each yo-yo. Sew a flower button only at the top of the remaining stem.

4. Using the leaf pattern on page 43, cut 4 leaves from the dark green washable felt. Stitch a leaf to each stem and tie the floppy leaf into a knot (see "Knotted Leaves" on page 16). "Work" the knots and fluff the leaves. You'll have 1 unknotted leaf left over.

DETAIL: BIB FRONT YO-YO FLOWER

FUSING AND EMBELLISHING THE BIB BACK

1. Place the remaining (intact) Log Cabin block in the center of the bib back as shown in the inset detail on page 35. Remember to keep the block clear of the bottom seam. Fuse, then stitch the detail block in place.

2. Tack and knot the remaining leaf in the center of the Log Cabin block. Sew the remaining flower button above the leaf.

MAKING BUTTON LOOPS AND FINISHING

1. To make button loops for the bib, cut the remaining piece of twine into 2 pieces, each 18" long, and cut 2 strips, each 1" x 18", from leftover flannel. Braid the flannel strips and twine into 1 long piece, using the 2 twine pieces as a single strand (see "Braiding" on page 15). Don't forget to stitch across the start and end of the braid when you finish braiding.

2. Mark the braid at 5" and again at 6" from the stitching along the top edge. Stitch across on those lines, then cut *between* them. Measure, mark, and cut to make a second button loop.

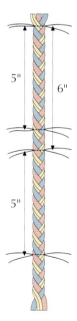

3. Position button loops on bib front as shown and baste in place. Be sure to keep the loops away from the underarm seam allowance.

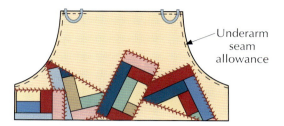

Braided loop placement

4. Follow the pattern directions to complete the assembly of your overalls. Instead of sewing buttons to the straps, I just tie the straps through the button loops.

COUNTRY COMFORTABLE: CHILD'S OVERALLS

MATERIALS: 42"-WIDE FABRIC

A favorite overalls pattern

Plush felt for bib section of overalls*

Print flannel for trouser section of overalls*

Contrasting flannel for bib lining, straps, and pockets*

9 pieces (⅛ yd. each) or assorted flannel scraps (totaling 1⅛ yds.) in coordinating colors for Log Cabin blocks and yo-yos

1 craft-size square of dark green washable felt (9" x 12") for leaves

¼ yd. of fusible web

2 pieces of jute twine, each 36" long

Assorted skeins of embroidery floss

3 porcelain flower buttons**

*Refer to the pattern packaging for the specific yardage in your child's size.

**See "Resources" on page 95. You may need additonal "plain" buttons if your pattern requires them for side closures.

DETAIL: CHILD'S OVERALLS, BIB FRONT

Note: *Refer to "Techniques, Terminology, and Tips" on pages 6–19 for guidance in preparing and assembling this garment.*

CUTTING OUT THE OVERALLS

Follow the adult overalls instructions for cutting out the fabrics for the child's overalls (see "Cutting Out the Overalls" on page 37).

MAKING THE LOG CABIN BLOCKS

1. Follow the adult overalls instructions to cut and assemble 2 Log Cabin blocks (see "Making the Log Cabin Blocks" on page 37). For the child's version, cut two 2½" center squares and eight 1½" strips of different colors and prints to make a block with 8 strips or "logs" as shown. The blocks should measure 6½" x 6½", including the seam allowance.

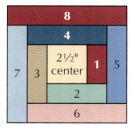

2. Continue with the adult overalls instructions by bonding the blocks to fusible web. Cut 1 of the Log Cabin blocks in half on the diagonal; then cut 1 of these halves in half again. Remove the paper back from the triangles. Lay the front bib section face up on the worktable. Arrange the 3 Log Cabin triangles as shown or to suit yourself. Fuse them in place and finish with a decorative stitch.

DETAIL: CHILD'S OVERALLS, BIB BACK

EMBELLISHING AND FINISHING

1. Cut 2 pieces of twine, one 11" and the other 7" long. Squiggle, pin, and stitch the stems in place on the bib as shown in the detail on page 41 (also see "Squiggle and Stitch" on page 17).

2. Follow the adult overalls instructions to complete the overalls. Make 2 yo-yo flowers and position them at the top of the twine stems. Stitch in place and add a button to the center of each flower. Make 3 green felt leaves, reserving 1 for the back. Stitch 2 to the front, knotting and fluffing them.

3. Finish the bib back with the remaining Log Cabin block, knotted leaf, and embellishing button as shown in the detail photo below. Finish the bib front with braided button loops. Follow your pattern instructions to complete the assembly of the overalls.

Country Comfortable Overalls
Templates

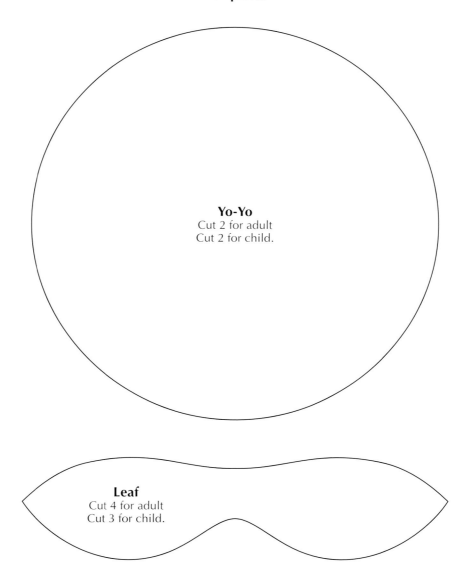

Yo-Yo
Cut 2 for adult
Cut 2 for child.

Leaf
Cut 4 for adult
Cut 3 for child.

SWEATSHIRT DRESSES

I know . . . I know! Sweatshirts have been decorated, and then decorated some more, in just about every way imaginable. But you must admit, a sweatshirt does make an easy, versatile canvas. What other "medium" is so easy to find, inexpensive to purchase, and comes in almost everyone's size and favorite color? What could be better for those days when you want to create something fast from materials at hand?

I think these mother/daughter sweatshirt dresses fill the bill perfectly. I suspect you have a few slightly used sweatshirts around the house and a fabric lover's stash of scraps, trims, and other baubles. Use them to make a garment just like mine, or one that incorporates your own favorite mother/daughter sayings and appliqués. Either way, you'll reach for these garments again and again—I guarantee!

THIS IS ME!: CHILD'S DRESS

Note: *Refer to "Techniques, Terminology, and Tips" on pages 6–19 for guidance in preparing and assembling this garment.*

PREPARING THE SWEATSHIRT

1. Refer to "Selecting and Preparing a Sweatshirt" on pages 9–11 for instructions on prewashing and preparation of the base garment. For this project, you'll need to remove the bottom ribbing and cuff ribbing. *Leave the neckline ribbing intact.*

2. Try the sweatshirt on the child and mark (or pin) at the desired waistline. This dress is intended as a modified "baby doll" look, so you'll want to raise the waistline slightly.

3. Remove the sweatshirt and cut away the excess fabric from the bottom.

4. Embroider the neckline seam with cross-stitches as seen in the detail at right (also see "Decorative Stitches" on page 16). Be careful not to draw up the fabric or you will lose the stretch in the neckline ribbing.

5. Straighten the raw edges of the sleeves if necessary. Turn up each sleeve 1½" to form a cuff and pin-baste. Sew a blanket stitch around the top of the cuff with a double length of embroidery floss as shown. Be sure to catch the sleeve in the stitch.

6. Embellish each cuff with 4 floss-tied wooden buttons.

CUFF DETAIL

FRONT DETAIL

EMBELLISHING THE SWEATSHIRT FRONT

1. Use a water-soluble marking pen to print or write the words "This is me!" as shown on the left side of the sweatshirt front. (Remember: you are looking at a photo, so the "left" becomes "right" when the garment is worn!) Use your most childlike lettering. Hand embroider or machine stitch over the words with contrasting embroidery floss or colorful decorative thread. I used my machine's satin stitch to make the letters.

2. Make a child's dress and apron template using the patterns on page 54. Bond and cut out the appliqués, then position them on the opposite side of the sweatshirt front (see "Fusible Web" on page 8 and "Using the Appliqué Patterns" on page 13). Do not fuse yet!

3. Cut 4 pieces of jute twine, each 4" long. Tuck 2 pieces under the shoulder area of the dress appli-qué and 2 pieces under the hem. Now fuse the dress and apron appliqués in place, then stitch around them with a decorative hand or machine stitch.

4. "Squiggle" the twine arms and legs as shown in the photo above; pin them in place. Stitch over each limb with a wide zigzag stitch (see "Squiggle and Stitch" on page 17).

5. Sew a wooden button to "dot" the exclamation point, and another at the end of each twine leg to create a foot. Use embroidery floss—all the strands!—and let the tails hang free. Stitch a porcelain theme button to the end of one twine arm for the hand, and a wooden button to the other.

6. Use the 2" square of cardboard to make the hair. Wind the cotton yarn around the cardboard 6 or 7 times and cut it off from the yarn ball.

7. Carefully remove the bundle from the cardboard. Next, cut a 6"-long piece of yarn from the ball and use it to tie the bundle in the center. Do not trim the tails! Repeat twice for a total of 3 "hair" bundles.

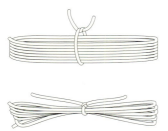

8. There are 5 holes in the primitive-face button. The 2 in the center are for sewing the button to the project. The remaining 3 are for adding the hair bundles. Moisten the tail of each bundle, and poke it through a hole. Tie into a knot with its opposite

tail; fluff. It will look like a "bad hair day." To tame the hair, cut a ½" x 8" strip of flannel. Tack it to the top of the hair, tie into a bow, and trim the ends to tame the bad-hair blues. Refer to the detail photo on page 45 for guidance.

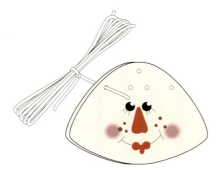

9. Stitch the "coiffed" face in place above the dress appliqué, and use embroidery floss to add a wooden button to the apron.

CONSTRUCTING AND ADDING THE SKIRT

1. Lay your skirt fabric, just as it came off the bolt, with selvages together, on your worktable. Smooth out, straighten the top and bottom cut edges if needed, and fold in half as shown to make 2 equal lengths. Mark the fold line and cut apart. These are your skirt lengths front and back. But wait! We need to determine the width of each piece.

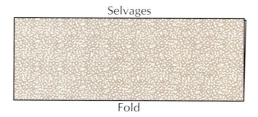

Selvages

Fold

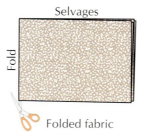

Selvages

Fold

Folded fabric

2. Place the sweatshirt bodice on the worktable and measure across the bottom edge. That measurement is _____ (your bodice width). Also mark the "side" seams of the sweatshirt with a pin. You will need this guideline later when you attach the skirt.

Pin   Measure here.   Pin
This is "your"
measurement.

3. Place 1 skirt length on the worktable, right side up and selvages together. At one end, mark your bodice-width measurement out from the fold. Repeat at the other end. Connect these marks down the length of the fabric, using a ruler and marking pen for a perfect line. With scissors or a rotary cutter, cut on the line. Add the excess fabric, if any, to your fabric stash. Repeat this process for the remaining skirt length.

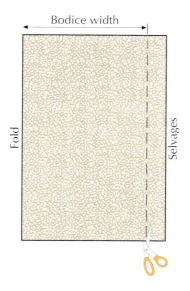

Bodice width

Fold

Selvages

4. Unfold, then place the skirt lengths RST; pin-baste, matching tops and bottoms. (Take care if you are using a directional fabric!) Stitch the sides lengthwise, using a ⅝"-wide seam allowance. Clean-finish or serge the seams if needed (see "Clean Finishing/Serging" on page 12).

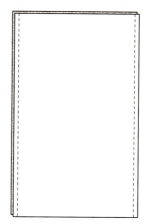

5. Gather one end of the skirt using your favorite gathering method. If you are using a directional print for your skirt, be sure to gather the correct end. In other words, you don't want the little cats' heads upside down!

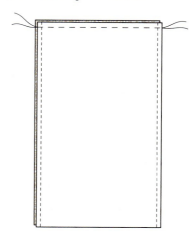

6. Place the gathered skirt and sweatshirt bodice RST as shown. Pin-baste the gathered edge of the skirt to the bottom edge of the sweatshirt, matching the side seams of the skirt to the pin marks on the bodice. Be careful not to pull the sweatshirt bodice out of shape. Stitch the gathered skirt in place, using a ⅝"-wide seam allowance. Serge or clean-finish the seam.

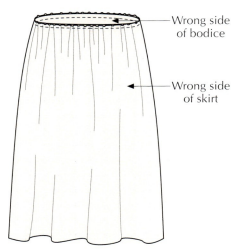

Wrong side of bodice

Wrong side of skirt

7. Clean-finish the hemline and turn up a 2" hem. Pin-baste the hem in place, machine stitch, and press. Or use your favorite hand method for hemming (see "Hems" on page 12).

PURSE DETAIL

ASSEMBLING AND ATTACHING THE POCKET PURSE

1. Make a template using the pocket-purse pattern on pages 56–57. Trace the template onto the wrong side of the purse fabric and cut out. Cut a 7" x 16" square of flannel for the lining.

2. Place the purse and lining RST and stitch around the outside edges, using a ¼"-wide seam allowance and leaving an opening on one side for turning. Press. Trim the excess fabric, clip corners and curves, then turn the purse right side out. Press again and hand stitch the opening closed.

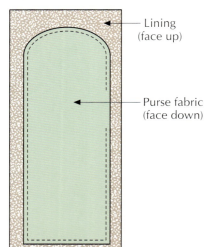

Lining (face up)

Purse fabric (face down)

3. Center a piece of the hook-and-loop fastener to the lining on the rounded end of the purse. Position it at least ¾" from the edge and stitch in place.

4. Fold the purse up 5" with the purse fabric—not the lining—exposed. Pin the purse together and mark the spot for the remaining piece of hook-and-loop fastener. Unpin the purse and sew the fastener in place.

5. Refold and pin the purse. Use a double length of embroidery floss and sew a blanket stitch or your favorite stitch all around the entire purse. Refer to the detail photo for guidance. Be sure to catch both the front and the back.

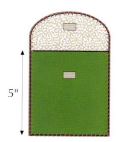

5"

6. Cut 2 pieces of jute twine, each 20" long, and 2 contrasting flannel strips, each ½" x 20". Braid the entire length, using the 2 pieces of twine as a single strand to form a handle for the purse (see "Braiding" on page 15). Machine or hand tack each end of the handle inside the purse near the back side seams.

7. Cut 2 pieces of jute twine, each 7" long, and tack them by hand or machine to either side of the purse back just below the flap fold. These will be used to attach the purse to the waistline of the dress.

8. Follow the instructions on the package to cover the 3 button forms with contrasting flannel fabric. Stitch 1 covered button in the center of the purse flap as shown on page 50.

9. Lay the dress face up on your worktable and position the purse at the waistline. Mark the placement of the twine ties right above the waistline seam.

Mark button placement.

10. Use the markings to stitch the remaining covered buttons in place.

11. Tuck the braided handle inside the purse; tie the twine tails in a bow around each of the covered buttons.

Purse back

AND THIS IS ME: ADULT DRESS

MATERIALS:
42"-WIDE FABRIC

A women's sweatshirt in your normal size with set-in sleeves for dress bodice

2½ yds. of flannel for skirt (all sizes)*

¼ yd. of contrasting flannel for purse and lining

Assorted flannel scraps for appliqués

Scraps of fusible web

Assorted skeins of embroidery floss

1 porcelain primitive-face button**

1 porcelain theme button for hand**

16 wooden buttons, ½" diameter

3 covered button forms, 1" diameter

Cotton yarn for hair

2" square of cardboard

2 yds. of jute twine

1" of sewable hook-and-loop fastener

Water-soluble marking pen

*Exact yardage will depend upon how long you want the skirt.

**Refer to "Resources" on page 95.

Note: *Refer to "Techniques, Terminology, and Tips" on pages 6–19 for guidance in preparing and assembling this garment.*

CONSTRUCTING AND EMBELLISHING THE DRESS

This garment is constructed in almost identical fashion to the child's dress. Follow the complete instructions for "This is Me!" on pages 47–51, with the following exceptions:

1. Mark and embroider the words "And This is Me" on the sweatshirt bodice. Embroider stars to dot the i's and omit the exclamation point.

2. Make templates for the dress and apron appliqués using the adult dress and apron patterns on page 54.

3. Stitch 6 wooden buttons around the cuff of each sleeve.

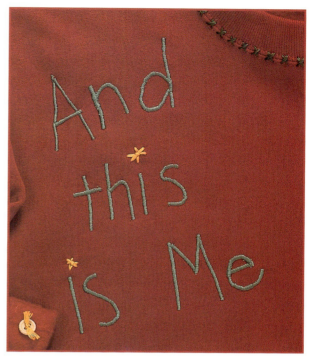

DETAIL: SWEATSHIRT BODICE

COMPANION PROJECT : BOY'S SWEATSHIRT

We can't leave the boys out! To adapt this pattern for your favorite little boy, make templates using the shirt and overalls patterns on page 55. Bond, cut, arrange, and fuse the appliqués in the center of an unaltered sweatshirt. Don't forget to position the twine arms and legs before you fuse the clothing appliqués in place. Add the button face, hands, and feet. Add a fused felt bow tie and a decorative shirt button to highlight his favorite hobby. I used a porcelain teddy bear, but you can choose your own embellishment.

Girl's Sweatshirt Dress
Templates

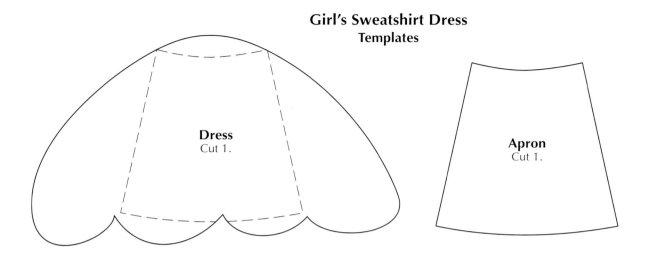

Dress
Cut 1.

Apron
Cut 1.

Adult Sweatshirt Dress
Templates

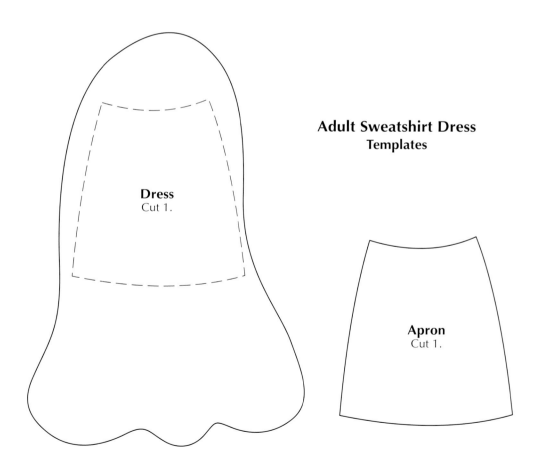

Dress
Cut 1.

Apron
Cut 1.

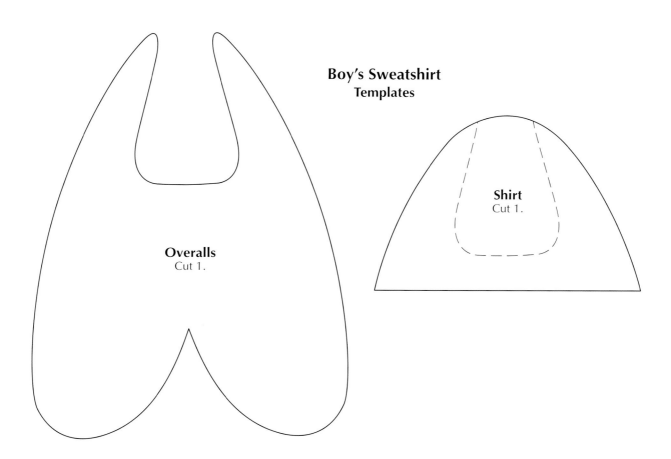

Boy's Sweatshirt
Templates

Overalls
Cut 1.

Shirt
Cut 1.

Sweatshirt Dress
Template

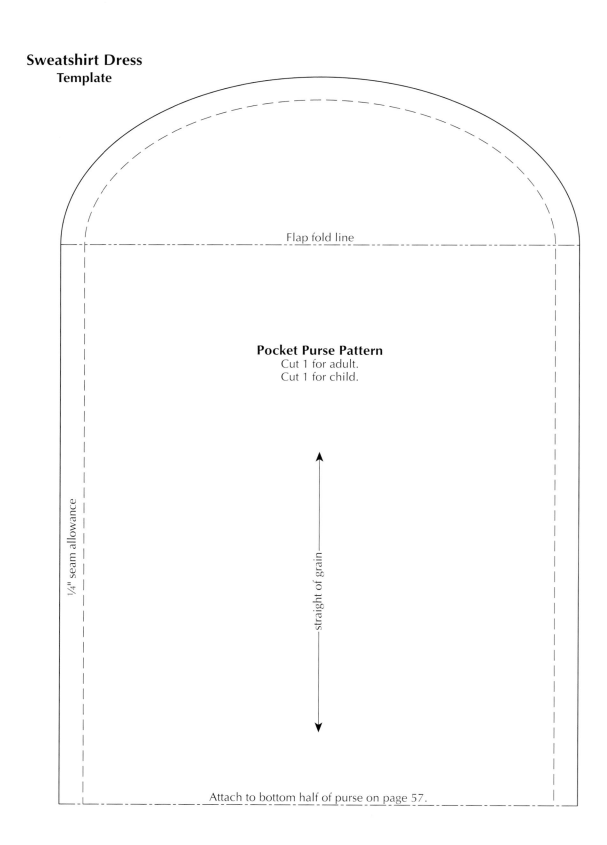

Flap fold line

Pocket Purse Pattern
Cut 1 for adult.
Cut 1 for child.

straight of grain

¼" seam allowance

Attach to bottom half of purse on page 57.

Sweatshirt Dress
Template

Attach to top half of purse on page 56.

Pocket Purse Pattern

Quik-Quilt™ Jackets

Memories . . . our lives are full of beautiful times that we would love to capture and hold forever. Fabric plays such an important part in those memories that it "wraps us up" in feelings. We remember the occasion for that special dress, the baby (who is now 25!) wearing her first delicately stitched kimono, a carefully embroidered scarf or hanky, and that magical "blankie" that kept all the monsters away.

I soon found myself thinking it would be fun to create a garment or two to celebrate precious fabric memories . . . and hence these Quik-Quilt™ jackets. I used reproduction fabrics and embroidered phrases to give the illusion of memorable milestones, but I urge you to substitute any fabrics, laces, or ribbons that hold lovely memories for you or a special someone. What better Mother's Day gift than a "memory jacket" with its own memory album to show the source of those vintage fabrics?

THE FABRIC OF MY LIFE: ADULT JACKET

MATERIALS: 42"-WIDE FABRIC

A men's sweatshirt with set-in sleeves

Solid-colored cotton fabric for patchwork blocks*

20 assorted reproduction prints or assorted scraps from vintage fabrics to coordinate with solid blocks**

1/8 yd. of a green reproduction print for folded leaves

1/8 yd. of a contrasting reproduction fabric for jacket binding

1 yd. of a contrasting reproduction fabric for sleeves

6 assorted skeins of colorful, contrasting embroidery floss

4 assorted colorful buttons, 1" diameter

Water-soluble marker

*1 1/8 yds. for small/medium; 1 1/4 yds. for large/extra large

**True 1/8-yd. cuts (4 1/2" x 42") for small/medium; true 1/4-yd. cuts (9" x 42") for large/extra large

Note: Refer to "Techniques, Terminology, and Tips" on pages 6–19 for guidance in preparing and assembling this garment.

The body of this sweatshirt-based jacket is constructed from "quilt-top fabric" that you'll piece yourself! Because sizes vary, you may need to add or subtract blocks as you stitch the garment together, but you needn't worry about that now. Remember to use ¼"-wide seam allowances as you piece the quilt-top fabric.

PREPARING AND ASSEMBLING THE JACKET

1. Select, prewash, and prepare the sweatshirt (see pages 9–11).

2. Using a rotary cutter, cut 6 strips, each 4½" x 42", from the solid-colored cotton. Crosscut these 6 strips into 52 squares, each 4½" x 4½", and set them aside. You may cut more as needed.

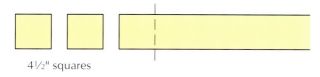

4½" squares

3. Cut 3 squares, each 4½" x 4½", from *each* of the ⅛- or ¼-yard pieces of reproduction fabrics.

4. Pair a 4½" solid square RST with a 4½" reproduction print square to make 16 pairs for chain piecing. Chain-piece the pairs; press the seam allowances open (see "Chain Piecing" on page 12). Pressing the seam allowances open makes it easier to match the many seams when piecing and reduces the overall bulk of the quilt-top fabric.

5. Lay out the chain-pieced units, arranging them in pairs to create four-patch units as shown. Experiment with color and fabric placement. When you are satisfied, stack the pairs RST for chain piecing.

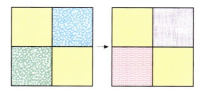

Place a pin along the seam to be stitched. This eliminates the confusion that always seems to happen on the way to the sewing machine!

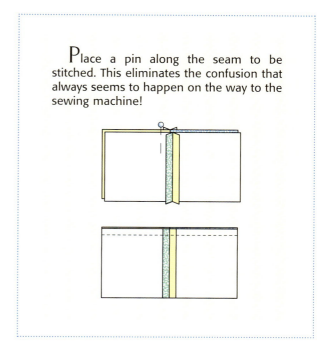

6. Chain-piece the pairs together. Clip the threads connecting the new four-patch units; press the seams open. You now have 8 four-patch units.

7. Arrange 2 four-patch units together as shown. Pin, stitch, and press the seams open. You now have a total of 4 units.

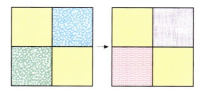

8. Pin, then stitch the larger units together to make one long length of quilt-top fabric. The new fabric measures 4 individual 4½" squares wide x 8 individual 4½" squares long. Press the seams open.

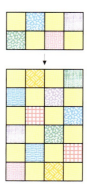

9. Lay the pieced fabric face down on your worktable. Place 1 sweatshirt front face down on the pieced fabric. You'll know immediately whether you need to add extra 4½" squares. Do any additional piecing now. The number of blocks here is based on a medium-sized jacket. Larger sizes will need more blocks.

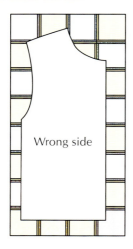

Wrong side

10. Smooth out wrinkles and pin-baste the 2 layers generously. Further secure the layers by stitching a scant ¼" from the edges with a machine basting stitch. Trim the excess pieced fabric from around the sweatshirt front and press the panel well.

11. Repeat for the remaining front panel and the back of the sweatshirt. (You'll need to join two 4-square x 16-square panels for the back.) Cut and piece additional 4½" squares as needed.

Machine Quilting the Jacket Body

1. Select a favorite decorative stitch to machine quilt the jacket pieces. For this project, I used my all-time favorite: the feather stitch (see detail photo on page 63). If your machine doesn't have a variety of fancy decorative stitches, play with the zigzag stitch. Adjust the stitch length and play on a scrap until you see an effect that catches your eye.

2. Start stitching at the top edge of one seam line and stitch down the center of that seam all the way

to the bottom edge (like stitching in-the-ditch). Try not to pull or stretch the piece while stitching, other than to smooth an errant wrinkle or pucker. Let your machine do the moving for you.

When you finish the first seam, sew off the fabric and clip the threads. Begin at the next seam line and stitch back to the top. Continue until you have quilted all of the top-to-bottom seams, then repeat to quilt the crosswise seams as well. Press the quilted panel carefully. If needed, give the panel a little squirt of starch to make it behave!

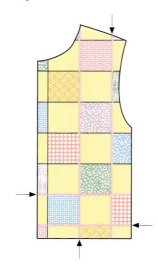

3. Repeat the quilting process for the remaining front panel and the jacket back. Try using different-colored quilting threads for an old-fashioned look.

Adding the Embroidered Sentiments

Time to write! (Now don't complain. The effect won't be the same if your notes are not in your very own handwriting.)

1. Use a water-soluble marker to fill as many 4½" solid squares as you like with meaningful dates, names, and occasions: "kitchen curtains—1953," "Mom's apron—1948," birthdays, anniversaries, and so on.

2. Use 2 strands of contrasting embroidery floss to embroider over the words in your favorite stitch as shown in the photo below.

DETAIL: EMBROIDERED PATCHES

EMBELLISHING THE JACKET BACK

1. Make a template using the yo-yo pattern on page 72. Cut 4 circles from leftover fabrics and make them into yo-yos (see "Yo-Yos" on page 17).

2. Cut 8 squares, each 4½" x 4½", from the green print fabric for the folded leaves. Fold them at your sewing machine so that you can baste each one as it is completed.

3. Place a square wrong side up and fold over one edge 1". Finger-press.

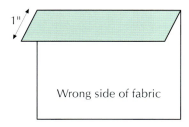

4. Fold the left corner down 2" as shown. Finger-press.

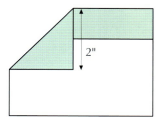

5. Fold the opposite corner down as shown.

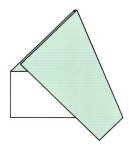

6. Fold the bottom left section over, leaving the previously folded fabric exposed 1".

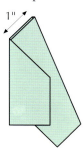

7. Fold the entire right section over the left to form the final fold. The resulting shape should resemble a folded "bud," though it is being used as a leaf. Place a pin through the center, if necessary, to hold it while machine basting as shown. After basting, cut away excess side fabric.

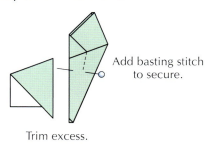

8. Repeat steps 3–7 to make 8 leaves.

9. Referring to the detail photo on page 59, arrange the leaves and yo-yo flowers on the jacket back. I arranged mine around a print block that happened to be right in the center, but you can scatter yours however you wish. Pin-baste each flower and leaf in place.

10. Thread your sewing machine with matching thread and stitch the leaves in place. A little straight stitch right under the fold works perfectly. You can temporarily remove the yo-yos if they are in the way.

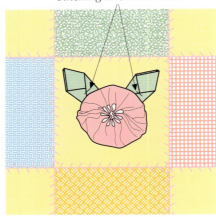

Stitching line *under* fold

11. Secure each yo-yo with a zigzag stitch, then use embroidery floss and a decorative button to embellish its center.

12. Use the water-soluble marker to draw tendrils around each yo-yo flower. Embroider the tendrils with contrasting embroidery floss.

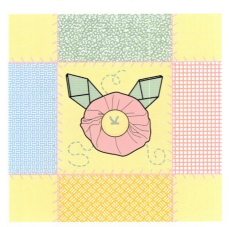

ASSEMBLING AND ATTACHING THE SLEEVES

1. Layer the reproduction sleeve fabric and each sweatshirt sleeve face down on your worktable. The sleeves can be placed on the fabric in any direction—unless you have a one-way print.

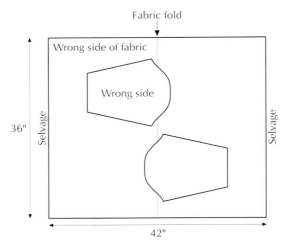

Fabric fold

Wrong side of fabric

Wrong side

36"

Selvage

Selvage

42"

Pin-baste the layers, then trim the excess reproduction fabric from around each sweatshirt sleeve. Use a long basting stitch to machine baste the layers together all around each sleeve. Press, then fold each sleeve in half lengthwise. Mark or place a pin at the center point, along the top edge of the sleeve.

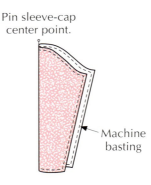

Pin sleeve-cap center point.

Machine basting

2. Mark a 2" quilting grid on each sleeve, then machine quilt with matching thread (see "Crosshatch Quilting" on page 19).

SLEEVE DETAIL

ASSEMBLING AND FINISHING THE JACKET

1. Place each front panel RST with the jacket back; pin and stitch at the shoulder seams, taking a generous ¼" seam allowance. Serge or clean-finish the seams (see "Clean Finishing/Serging" on page 12. With RST, match each sleeve's marked center to the shoulder seam; stitch, serge, and press.

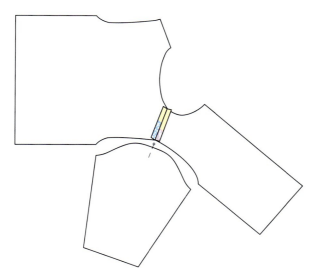

2. Join the underarm and side jacket seam, beginning at the bottom edge of the jacket and continuing down the sleeve to the cuff area. Serge and press.

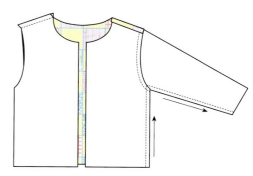

3. Use a plate or a dressmaker's curve to gently round the neckline and the bottom edge of the jacket's front panels.

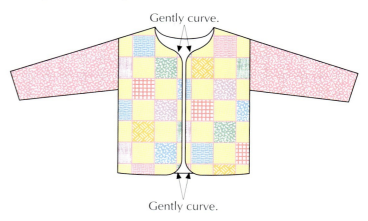

Gently curve.

Gently curve.

4. Cut 3 binding strips, each 1½" x 42", from the contrasting binding fabric. (The crosswise grain has enough give to handle the gentle curves.) Sew the strips together to make one continuous strip; apply the binding to the jacket edges and sleeves (see "Making and Applying Bindings" on pages 14–15).

BINDING DETAIL

I REMEMBER: CHILD'S JACKET

MATERIALS: 42"-WIDE FABRIC

A boy's sweatshirt with set-in sleeves, slightly larger than the child would normally wear

True ⅛-yd. cuts (4½" x 42") or assorted large scraps of 15 reproduction print and solid cotton fabrics

⅛ yd. or a large scrap of contrasting fabric for jacket binding

1 yd. of fusible web

2 spools of same-color thread for decorative stitching

Assorted skeins of embroidery floss

1 colored button, 1" diameter

This is really fast and fun and a good way to use small yardages and leftover scraps. I used an assortment of blue prints and yellow prints on one front. For the remaining front, I chose pinks and greens.

Note: Refer to "Techniques, Terminology, and Tips" on pages 6–19 for guidance in preparing and assembling this garment.

PREPARING AND FUSING THE SWEATSHIRT

1. Select, prewash, and prepare the sweatshirt (see "Selecting and Preparing a Sweatshirt" on pages 9–11). Do *not* remove the ribbed sleeve cuffs.

2. Bond an assortment of the ⅛-yard cuts or scraps of prints and solids to fusible web (see "Fusible Web" on page 8). Cut the fused fabric into 4½" squares. Start with 3 of each color and add more as needed.

3. Place one of the sweatshirt's front panels face up on the ironing board. Cut a rectangle, triangle, or other shape from a randomly selected 4½" fused square. Remove the paper backing and place the shape right in the center of the panel. Cut a few more different shapes from other fabrics, and position them around the initial shape, slightly overlapping the raw edges. Fuse the shapes into place.

Keep cutting and placing fused shapes until the entire front panel is filled. (Just try to make a boo-boo with this technique!) Refer to the photo on page 66 for inspiration.

4. Thread your machine with 2 spools of the same-color thread. Sew a decorative stitch around each of the fused shapes. Do not overlap the stitching from shape to shape. Instead, backstitch and move on. Clip any errant threads and press. Repeat steps 3 and 4 to construct the other front panel.

5. Use the same method to cut, bond, arrange, and fuse random shapes on the back of the sweatshirt. Position the "starter" shape at the midpoint along the bottom edge, and arrange succeeding shapes outward from this center mark. Try not to go higher than 4" from the jacket's bottom edge. Finish each shape with decorative stitching.

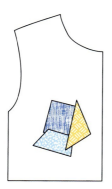

DETAIL: BACK BOTTOM EDGE

6. Cut a solid 4½" square and bond it with fusible web. Center the square approximately 2" below the back neckline as shown in the detail photo. Fuse the square to the sweatshirt and add decorative stitching.

DETAIL: BACK TOP EDGE

EMBELLISHING THE JACKET BACK

1. Make a template using the yo-yo pattern on page 72, and make a single yo-yo from leftover fabric (see "Yo-Yos" on page 17).

2. Cut 2 print fabric squares, each 4½" x 4½", for the folded leaves. Refer to the instructions for the adult jacket for assistance in folding the leaf fabric (see "Embellishing the Jacket Back," steps 2–7, on page 63).

3. Continue following the instructions for "The Fabric of My Life" to position and attach the yo-yo flower and folded leaves in the center of the fused square. Finish with decorative stitching and a button as suggested.

ASSEMBLING AND ATTACHING THE SLEEVES

1. Slip each sleeve on a "willing" child and mark the elbow. Carefully cut away the seam to approximately 1" from the ribbed cuff.

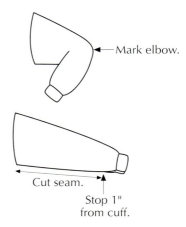

Mark elbow.

Cut seam.

Stop 1" from cuff.

2. Lay each sleeve face up on the ironing board. Cut and bond 4 or 5 shapes cut from 4½" squares for each sleeve. Arrange them over the elbow marks, fusing and stitching around each shape as before.

SLEEVE DETAIL

ASSEMBLING AND FINISHING THE JACKET

Assemble the jacket in the same manner as the adult jacket (see "Assembling and Finishing the Jacket" on page 65). Use the ribbed cuffs to line up the original sleeve seams, tapering as necessary. Start at the cuffed edge to resew the seams. Finish by rounding the corners of the jacket front, then making and attaching a contrasting binding (see "Making and Applying Bindings" on pages 14–15.).

COMPANION PROJECTS: DOLL PURSE

Note: *Refer to "Techniques, Terminology, and Tips" on pages 6–19 for guidance in assembling this project.*

ASSEMBLING THE PURSE

1. Cut 2 rectangles, each 11" x 18", from fabric for the dress. Place them RST and stitch down each long side and across the bottom edge. Leave an opening on each side to insert the arms.

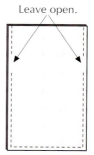

2. Turn down the unsewn edge 1" to form a casing and stitch, leaving an opening for the gathering string.

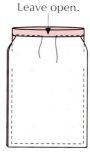

3. Run the 12"-long elastic or string through the casing, using a safety pin or other casing gadget, but do not gather it; just secure it to the opening.

4. Cut 2 fabric strips, each 4" x 11", for sleeves, and 2 pieces, each 4" x 4", from skin-colored fabric for the arms. Place a sleeve and an arm strip RST along a short edge; sew to make 1 arm unit, and press. Sew the other arm unit in the same manner.

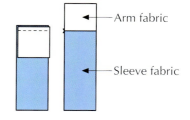

MATERIALS

Assorted fabric scraps for dress, apron, body, hands, face, kerchief, etc.

12" of narrow elastic or string for gathering

5" of hook-and-loop fastener

Small amount of Fairfield Poly-Fil batting

Permanent marking pens for drawing facial features

Glue gun

1 yd. of ribbon for apron ties

Assorted skeins of embroidery floss

Assorted buttons for embellishment

5. Fold the new strips RST lengthwise and stitch, leaving the short sleeve end of the unit open for turning. Turn the arm units right side out and press.

6. Insert an arm unit (sleeve first) into each of the dress openings and stitch through all layers to secure the arms in place.

7. Fold the bottom edge of the skirt up 6" to form a pouch; use pins or a water-soluble marker to mark on each side where the top edge lies. Using the marks for guidance, stitch hook-and-loop fastener to the pouch.

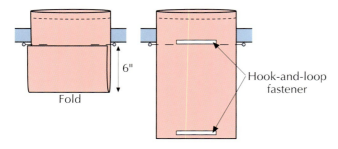

6"

Fold

Hook-and-loop fastener

8. Refold and pin-baste the dress to make the pouch permanent. Stitch down each side close to the edge with a decorative stitch. On the inside of the pouch, fold the bottom seam to form a tri-angle; stitch across the triangle on the inside of the purse to create a bottom.

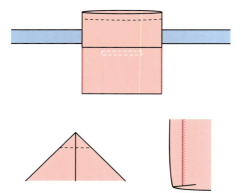

9. Make a template using the doll body pattern on page 73. Use skin-colored fabric to cut a front and back body piece. Place the pieces RST; stitch, leaving an opening, then turn the doll's head and upper body right side out. Stuff it tightly with Poly-Fil; stitch the opening closed.

10. Use permanent marking pens to draw and color the doll's facial features. Insert the body into the dress. Gather the dress at the neck by pulling snuggly on the elastic or string. Tie off and stitch the casing closed.

EMBELLISHING AND FINISHING THE PURSE

1. Refer to the photo on page 69 for embell-ishing ideas. Cut a 4" fabric scrap, fold into a head kerchief, and hot-glue it in place. Embellish the kerchief with ribbons or embroidery floss.

2. Cut a 6½" x 9½" rectangle and a 3" x 4" rectangle from contrasting fabrics for an apron. Join the 2 pieces so that the smaller one looks like the apron bib. (You can hem and embellish the apron as you wish.) Cut a 15" length of ribbon for the waistband and apron strings, then center and baste it to the apron. Cut a 5" length of ribbon and stitch each end to the top of the apron bib. Embellish this neck tie with buttons or beads.

3. Slip the apron over the doll's head and tie the apron strings so that the apron covers the pouch.

4. Tack the hands together and cover the join with a yo-yo or button. Then tack the sleeves to the kerchief so the head stays erect.

STRAW HAT

Hats are so easy to decorate . . . and they are so much fun!

1. Measure the straw hat around the crown. Add 3" to this measurement.

2. Cut a strip of solid-colored cotton 4½" wide and the length of your crown measurement.

3. Bond fabric squares of different colors and prints to fusible web, then cut the squares into various shapes.

4. Arrange and fuse the shapes to the cotton band, then finish each shape with decorative stitching. Turn under the lengthwise edge of the band ¾"; press and stitch close to each edge with a decorative stitch.

5. Place the decorated band around the crown of the hat, overlapping the ends, and hot-glue it in place.

Embellish the join with yo-yo flowers, folded leaves, and buttons. You're all set for "doing lunch!"

MATERIALS

Plain straw hat

Assorted scraps of pastel and reproduction fabrics

Scraps of fusible web

Glue gun

Assorted yo-yo flowers, folded leaves, and buttons

HEADBAND

Inexpensive plastic headbands can be spiffed up in a jiffy! Hot-glue yo-yo flowers and folded leaves to the center of the band as a treat for someone special.

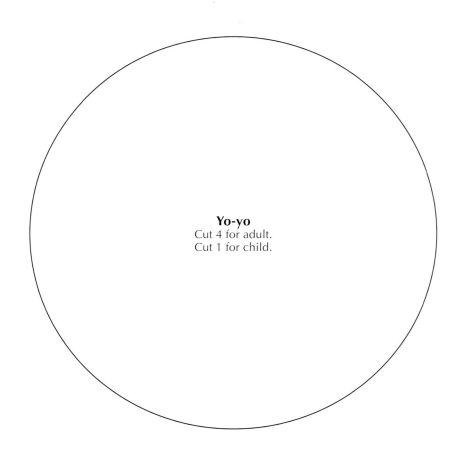

Yo-yo
Cut 4 for adult.
Cut 1 for child.

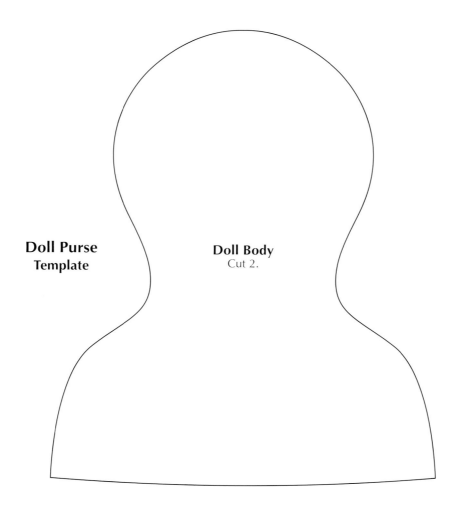

Doll Purse
Template

Doll Body
Cut 2.

FLEECE 'N FLANNEL JACKETS

F leece! The last time there was this much hype over a fabric, we were all a lot younger, looking cool in our leisure suits, and we called the fabric polyester. Some of polyester's most exciting attributes have carried over to fleece: easy care, no fraying edges, and lots of fun colors and prints. I know that you will want to try your hand at working with this miracle fabric.

To get you started, I have used a simple jacket pattern and added snazzy touches, such as oversized flannel Log Cabin pockets with rag fringe and a matching patchwork collar. Twine stems, chubby braided flowers, and easy felt leaves give the garment its trademark 3-dimensional look. Embellishments lend a garment that extra spice and show off the creativity of the maker.

As you work on this jacket, play with felt cutouts, porcelain buttons, and various trims. Don't ever be too timid to add your personal stamp of creativity. You can do it!

A WILDFLOWER WINTER: ADULT JACKET

MATERIALS

A favorite loose-fitting jacket pattern with round collar and roll-up cuffs

Fleece or Berber fabric*

Coordinating lining fabric if desired*

⅛-yd. cuts or assorted large scraps of at least 15 different flannel fabrics

1 yd. of rag fringe**

Contrasting embroidery floss

1 ball of medium jute twine

1 craft-size square of dark green washable felt (9" x 12") for leaves

3 covered button forms, 1" diameter

3 wooden buttons, ½" diameter

*Refer to the pattern packaging for the specific yardage in your size.

**See "Resources" on page 95

Note: Refer to "Techniques, Terminology, and Tips" on pages 6–19 for guidance in preparing and assembling this garment.

CUTTING OUT THE JACKET

Using the pattern pieces from the jacket pattern, cut out the jacket fronts, back, and sleeves from the fleece and lining fabric (if using).

ASSEMBLING AND ATTACHING THE LOG CABIN POCKETS

1. Look through your assorted flannels and decide on a fabric for the center square of the Log Cabin pockets. Cut 2 squares, each 2½" x 2½", from this fabric, and 1 strip, 1½" x 42", from each of the remaining flannels. If your fabric is not a full 42" wide, cut it so it yields the greatest possible length.

2. Assemble 2 Log Cabin blocks, using the 2½" flannel squares for the centers, and the 1½"-wide strips for the logs. Use the diagram as a guide for positioning the strips (see "Constructing Log Cabin Blocks" on page 14). Each block uses 14 strips around the center square and measures approximately 9½" x 9½", including the seam allowance.

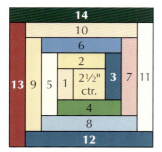

Log Cabin Pocket Block

3. Sew the 2 completed Log Cabin blocks together as shown to make 1 pocket unit; press.

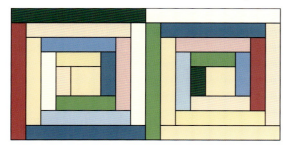

Log Cabin Pocket Unit

4. Lay the left front jacket panel on your work surface. (Remember: you are looking at a photo, so the left front jacket panel is actually on the right in the photo!) Position the pocket unit at the bottom edge as shown opposite. Depending on the jacket size, you may need to trim or add extra Log Cabin strips. If you need to add, now is the time to do it! To trim for smaller sizes, position the pocket unit to its best advantage and cut away the excess. After determining the fit, cut a piece of lining fabric the same size as the pocket unit. Set the lining aside.

DETAIL: LEFT FRONT JACKET PANEL

5. Cut a piece of rag fringe the same length as the top edge of the pocket unit. Align the seamed edge of the rag fringe with the top edge, (both right side up); pin, then machine stitch in place.

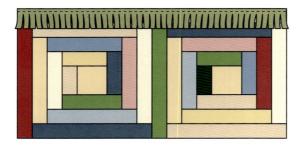

6. Pin the pocket and pocket lining RST, carefully pushing the fringe away from the seam area. Stitch the lining to the pocket along the 2 short sides and the fringe side, leaving the remaining long side unsewn. Turn the pocket right side out. Press near the seam, but take care not to press the fringe flat.

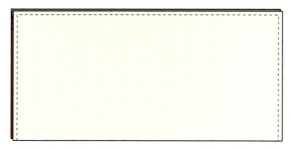

Leave open.

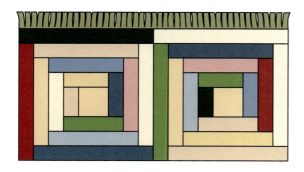

7. Embroider large cross-stitches across the pocket top with contrasting embroidery floss.

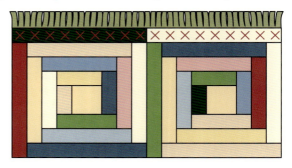

8. Position the pocket on the left front panel once again and pin-baste. Machine baste the 2 sides and bottom edge of the pocket to the front a scant ¼" from the edge. Find the center point of the pocket and stitch from the top to the bottom edge to form 2 pockets.

EMBELLISHING THE JACKET

1. Cut 3 pieces of twine in various lengths for stems on your fabric flowers. I used pieces 20", 23", and 24" long.

2. Use the squiggle-and-stitch method to secure the stems to the jacket (see "Squiggle and Stitch" on page 17). Tuck the starting end of the middle stem behind the rag fringe in the center of the pocket. Squiggle the stem upward, pinning as you go. Secure the stem in place with a wide zigzag stitch, remembering to remove the pins. Repeat to position and secure the remaining 2 stems. Let the stems fall over the edges of the Log Cabin pocket as shown in the photo, and squiggle away!

POCKET DETAIL

3. Make a template using the leaf pattern on page 85. Cut 4 leaves from the green washable felt. Refer to the detail photo on page 77 and place 1 leaf atop two stems and another along a stem as shown. Zigzag a few stitches in the center; tie and arrange the leaves. Stitch the remaining leaf to the top of the remaining stem and fold it as shown.

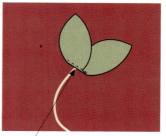

Stitch here.

Stitch here.

Folded leaf

4. To make the braided flowers, cut 2 pieces of twine 36" long, and 2 narrow strips of contrasting flannel 36" long. Arrange and braid the strands, using the 2 pieces of twine as a single strand (see "Braiding" on page 15).

5. Mark the braid 8" and 9" from the starting edge and stitch on the lines. Cut the braid apart between the 2 lines of stitching. Thread a regular sewing needle with a double length of knotted, matching thread. Coil the 8" length of braid to form a chubby flower. Tuck the end under; stitch on the underside, sewing each row to the next.

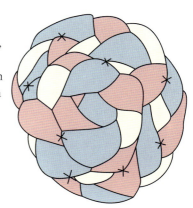

6. Make an additional flower, varying the length of the cut braid to change the size of the flower. Remember to make stitching lines on either side of your measurement before cutting so your braid won't unravel. Secure the flowers on top of the stems above the leaves as shown in the photo on page 77.

7. To make a fringe flower, cut a 1½"-long piece of rag fringe and curl it into a circle to resemble a zinnia. Pin-baste to hold, then place it above the remaining stem. Machine stitch it in place.

8. Cut 2 twine stems, each 24" long. Squiggle and pin-baste these stems to the right front jacket panel. Refer to the full-view photo on page 76 for guidance. I've wound one from the shoulder to the front center of the panel, and started another at the armhole area. Arrange as desired and cut off any excess. Don't feel that you need to use the entire length of twine. Make and add a braided flower, fringe flower, and 3 leaf sets to complete this side of the jacket. Refer once again to the photo on page 76 for guidance.

9. Use the same techniques to make and add vines, flowers, and leaves to the back right shoulder. Let the stems squiggle toward the center of the jacket back as shown in the photo below.

BACK DETAIL

CONSTRUCTING THE COLLAR

1. You'll need 2 extra-large Log Cabin blocks for the collar. These blocks must be large enough for the collar pattern to fit when placed diagonally. Cut 2 squares, each 2½" x 2½", from leftover flannel strips for the center squares. Use 1½"-wide flannel strips left over from the pocket to begin; cut additional strips as needed (you'll need to repeat a few). Begin with 20 strips or "logs," check against the collar pattern, and adjust the block size as needed (see "Constructing Log Cabin Blocks" on page 14).

2. The jacket pattern directions will most likely recommend that the collar pattern be placed on the fabric fold. Ignore this instruction. Instead, add a ¼"-wide seam allowance to the collar at the fold line. I suggest that you tape a paper extension to the pattern to represent the new cutting line and *recut* this new, enlarged pattern for cutting the collar pieces. This is no time for mistakes!

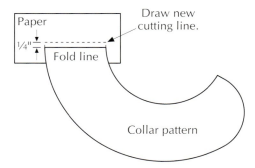

COLLAR DETAIL

3. Place the 2 Log Cabin blocks RST. Position the collar pattern with the new cutting line diagonally on the block. Cut the collar pieces. Place the collar pieces RST and stitch at the new seam allowance. Press the collar seam open.

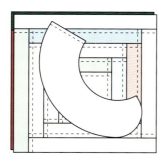

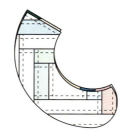

4. Cut a piece of lining fabric slightly larger than the open collar piece. Place the lining fabric and the collar RST. Stitch around the outside edge of the collar, using a ⅝" seam allowance. Leave the inside neck area unsewn. Trim away the excess fabric, clip the curves, turn the collar right side out, and press. (This method gives you more control when sewing around curves. You won't turn the piece right side out and find you haven't caught the seam!)

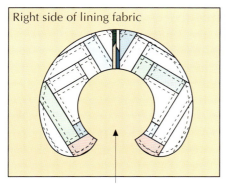

Leave neck area open.

ASSEMBLING AND FINISHING THE JACKET

1. Follow your pattern guidelines to assemble the jacket and lining.

2. Follow the packaging instructions to cover 3 button forms with leftover flannel. Sew the covered buttons to the right front panel in a vertical row, beginning about ½" from the neckline. Space the remaining buttons 1" apart.

3. Mark and stitch buttonholes on the left front panel.

4. Sew a prairie stitch around the jacket edges and collar with contrasting embroidery floss if desired (see "Prairie Stitch" on page 16). Refer to the photos on pages 76 and 80 for guidance.

5. Use contrasting embroidery floss to sew wooden buttons to the center of the fringe flowers.

DOWN LOG CABIN LANE: CHILD'S JACKET

MATERIALS

A favorite loose-fitting child's jacket pattern with round collar and roll-up cuffs

Fleece or Berber fabric*

Coordinating fabric for lining if desired*

⅛-yd. cuts or assorted large scraps of at least 12 different flannel fabrics

1 yd. of rag fringe**

Contrasting embroidery floss

1 ball of medium jute twine

1 craft-size square of dark green washable felt (9" x 12") for leaves

3 covered button forms, 1" diameter

3 wooden buttons, ½" diameter

1 pin clasp

Hot-glue gun (optional)

*Refer to the pattern packaging for the specific yardage in your child's size.

**See "Resources" on page 95.

CUTTING OUT THE JACKET AND ASSEMBLING THE LOG CABIN BLOCKS

1. Follow the instructions for the adult version of "Fleece 'n Flannel" to cut the jacket and lining pieces. The 2 Log Cabin blocks are constructed essentially the same, except the blocks are a bit smaller, requiring only 11 strips (or "logs") and measuring 7½" x 8½", including the seam allowance. Sew the 2 Log Cabin blocks together to make a 2-block unit as shown. Test the size of the pocket on the jacket front and add additional side rows if needed.

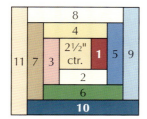

Log Cabin Pocket Block

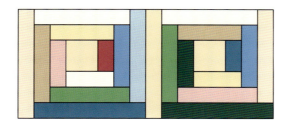

Log Cabin Pocket Unit

Continue to follow the adult jacket instructions to line, attach, and embellish the Log Cabin pockets (see "Cutting Out the Jacket" on page 77 and "Assembling and Attaching the Log Cabin Pockets" on pages 77–78).

EMBELLISHING THE JACKET

1. Cut 2 pieces of jute twine in different lengths. These will be the stems for the fabric flowers and leaves. I cut the stems 11" and 14", but you can make them any length you like.

2. Follow the squiggle-and-stitch instructions for the adult version of "Fleece 'n Flannel." Position and attach the vines to the front panels of the child's jacket (see "Embellishing the Jacket" on page 78). Refer to the photo on page 82 for guidance.

3. You can also refer to the adult instructions to make and attach 1 tied and 1 folded leaf, and 1 braided and 1 rag fringe flower for the left front panel of this pint-sized garment. (A separate flower pin goes on the right, but we'll get to that later.)

4. A decorative Log Cabin pocket graces the back of this garment. Use leftover 1½" flannel strips to sew together a Log Cabin block with a 2½" center square and 8 strips or "logs."

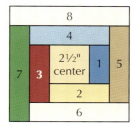

Log Cabin Back Pocket Square

BACK DETAIL

5. To finish the pocket, cut a 7" piece of rag fringe. Attach the fringe to the pocket as before. Cut a piece of lining fabric slightly larger than the Log Cabin block. Place the block and the lining RST. Stitch around the pocket, rounding out the 2 bottom corners and leaving an opening along one side for turning. Trim and clip curve; turn. Hand stitch the side opening closed and press.

6. Use embroidery floss to sew tiny cross-stitches across the pocket top.

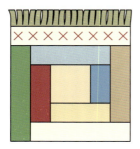

7. Center the pocket on the back of the jacket, approximately 11" from the neckline. Pin the pocket in place, then stitch close to the pocket edge with a decorative machine stitch; press.

8. Follow the package instructions to cover 3 button forms with leftover flannel. Add a prairie stitch along the inside edge of the pocket if desired. Make and add a knotted leaf and 1 covered button to the upper part of the pocket. Refer to the detail photo on page 83 for guidance.

9. Squiggle and stitch 3 additional stems to the back of the jacket, letting the stems fall inside the pocket. Make and add 2 more braided flowers, a fringe flower, and both a tied and folded leaf set.

FINISHING THE JACKET

1. Follow your pattern instructions for assembling the jacket with the lining. Don't forget to press.

2. Use contrasting embroidery floss to add prairie stitches all around the jacket edges (see "Prairie Stitch" on page 16).

3. Turn back the jacket fronts as shown in the photo. Lightly press, then pin-baste them in place.

4. Sew a flannel-covered button to each of the turned-back flaps.

NECKLINE DETAIL

MAKING THE DECORATIVE PIN

Make a template using the yo-yo pattern on page 85, and make 2 yo-yos from leftover lining fabric (see "Yo-Yos" on page 17). Fashion several braided and fringe flowers, using leftovers, and cut several leaf sets from extra felt. Cut a piece of felt 1½" x 2½" as a base

Refer to the pin detail photo below. Using the felt rectangle as a base, add the yo-yos, flowers, and leaves with embroidery floss or decorative buttons. Hot-glue or sew a pin clasp to the back of the yo-yo base, and pin the "corsage" to the right jacket front.

PIN DETAIL

COMPANION PROJECT : FLEECE HAT

Hats are back in style . . . hooray! When you make a new jacket or dress, why not design your own millinery masterpiece from leftover scraps? Find a simple hat pattern in a style becoming to you. I used fleece and lining left over from my "Fleece 'n Flannel" jacket to construct my hat. For embellishment, I did a prairie stitch around the brim with contrasting embroidery floss. Then I created a few flowers and leaves, folded up the brim, and tacked it in place with my floral creations. Not only cute, but it will protect my ears from winter's chill!

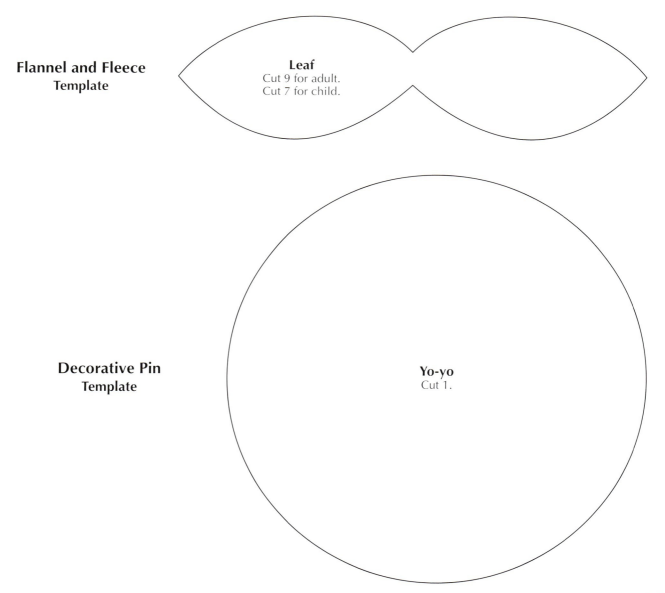

Flannel and Fleece
Template

Leaf
Cut 9 for adult.
Cut 7 for child.

Decorative Pin
Template

Yo-yo
Cut 1.

QUIK-QUILT™: SWEATSHIRT JACKETS

Sometimes when sewing or crafting, we get so involved in what's new out there, that we forget about those humble, but always faithful fabrics. Plain ol' washable felt is one of those "old faithfuls." You need only to pick up a pair of scissors to transform it into a useful project. Add decorative threads, trims, or buttons or fuse it to another fabric, and you are on your way to a masterpiece! I combined our wonderful Quik-Quilt™ technique with scraps of colorful fused felt to embellish these whimsical boy's and girl's jackets. Only the appliqués and embellishments differ. Use a bit of floss here and a little button there, and I think you'll agree that these jackets are both charming—and quick!

PLAYTIME:
BOY'S AND GIRL'S JACKETS

A boy's or girl's sweatshirt with set-in sleeves, one size larger than the child normally wears

Denim*

1/4 yd. of flannel for shirt, sleeves, and binding

Assorted colorful washable felt scraps for appliqués

Assorted skeins of embroidery floss

Assorted colorful buttons

1/4 yd. of fusible web

1/4 yd. of rag fringe or yarn for hair**

24" of jute twine, cut into one 6" and two 8" pieces

*Extra Small (2) or Small (3–4): 3/4 yd.; Medium (5–6) or Large (7–8): 7/8 yd.

**You'll need only about 3" for the boy's hair.

Note: *Refer to "Techniques, Terminology, and Tips" on pages 6–19 for guidance in preparing and assembling this garment.*

PREPARING THE SWEATSHIRT AND APPLIQUÉS

1. Select, prewash, and prepare the sweatshirt (see "Selecting and Preparing a Sweatshirt" on pages 9–11). You will be quilting and embellishing only the body of the sweatshirt (the front and back), so set the sleeves aside. You do not need to remove the ribbed cuffs.

2. Make templates for the appropriate appliqués using the patterns on pages 92–94. Bond scraps of washable felt in assorted colors to fusible web (see "Fusible Web" on page 8).

3. Trace and cut required appliqués from fused felt scraps as listed below (see "Using the Appliqué Patterns" and "Working with Fusibles" on pages 13 and 14).

For the boy's jacket, cut: 1 each of the face, ball cap and wedge, kite, overalls, pocket, boy's collar and cuff, pinwheel center, regular and reverse hand, and regular and reverse copter blade; 2 eyes; and 4 pinwheels.

For the girl's jacket, cut: 1 each of the face, girl's hat, kite, dress, heart, girl's collar and cuff, pinwheel center, flower, and regular and reverse hand; 2 eyes; and 4 pinwheels.

Set the appliqués aside for now.

4. Lay the denim fabric right side down on your work surface. Place the sweatshirt front panels and back right sides down on the denim. Leave a little extra fabric between each piece, smooth, and pin. Include a little extra denim as you cut around each sweatshirt piece. (This extra fabric makes it easier to machine baste the pieces together.) Machine baste around the pieces, keeping close to the edge. Press and trim away the excess denim.

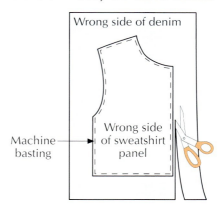

5. Quik-Quilt™ the back and 2 front panels with free-motion machine quilting (see "Free-Motion Quilting" on page 18). Lightly press each piece after quilting.

ASSEMBLING AND EMBELLISHING THE JACKET BACK

1. Straighten the jacket bottom with a rotary cutter if necessary. Make a mark 4½" up from the bottom on each side of the jacket back and measure across its width. Cut a piece of flannel 4½" wide and the length of your measurement.

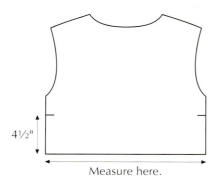

4½"

Measure here.

2. Align the flannel with the bottom edge of the jacket back, and pin it in place between the guide marks. Stitch across the top of the flannel with a decorative stitch; press. Smooth the layers, then pin and machine baste the side and bottom edges. This creates the boy's shirt or the girl's blouse.

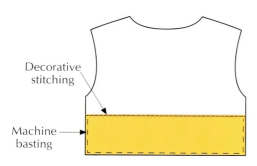

Decorative stitching

Machine basting

3. Halve the measurement you used for the flannel strip to find and mark the midpoint on the back of the shirt or blouse. Center the face snugly over the shirt or blouse on the back of the jacket, using the placement marks as a guide. Fuse, and stitch around the face with a decorative stitch.

4. Fuse and stitch the eyes to the center of the face, "snugging" the eyes to the edge of the shirt or blouse. Refer to the photos on this page for guidance.

5. Position the ball cap or girl's hat at an angle over the face. Tuck a piece of rag fringe or yarn hair under the cap or hat, and one end of the 6" piece of jute twine under the top of the cap or

hat. Fuse the hat or cap with contrasting cap wedge in place and finish with a decorative stitch.

6. "Squiggle" and pin the twine toward the shoulder area of the jacket, then secure the twine with a wide zigzag stitch (see "Squiggle and Stitch" on page 17). Place the copter blades or flower over the end of the twine in any direction you like; fuse and stitch down.

7. Place, fuse, and stitch the collar under the face, the overalls or dress under the collar (but over the flannel shirt or blouse!), and the pocket in the center of the overalls or the heart in the center of the dress.

8. Add embroidery to the cap or hat and overalls or dress. Attach 2 buttons to the shirt or blouse front, 1 as the center of the copter blades or flower, and 1 to the top of the cap or hat.

BOY'S BACK

GIRL'S BACK

Assembling and Embellishing the Jacket Front

1. Cut 2 pieces of flannel, each 2½" x 4½". Mark the 2 side edges of each front panel 4½" from the bottom edge, just as you did for the back. Align a flannel piece to the bottom edge of each front panel within the marked guidelines. Stitch across the top inner edge of the flannel pieces with a decorative stitch, and around the outside and bottom with a straight basting stitch.

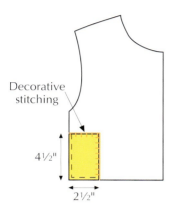

Decorative stitching

4½"

2½"

2. Place the felt cuffs over each sleeve, slightly overlapping the flannel. "Snug" a hand next to the cuff. You can vary the placement of the hands if you like: 1 up and 1 down. Tuck an 8" piece of twine under the fingers and over the thumb of each hand. Fuse the cuffs and hands in place; stitch.

3. Squiggle and stitch over the twine on both fronts using the photos on page 88 as a guide.

4. Fuse and stitch the kite over the end of the twine on the left front panel. (Remember: you are looking at a photo, so the left front panel is actually on the right in the photo.) Cut 2 crossbars freehand from leftover fused felt and fuse them onto the kite. Cut 2 pieces of unfused felt, each ½" x 5", for kite tails. Place these on the kite string, tack in place, and tie knots. Add a button to the center of the kite with embroidery floss.

5. Fuse and stitch the pinwheel pieces to the end of the twine on the right front panel. Fuse and stitch the circle to the center of the pinwheel; add a button to the center with embroidery floss.

DETAIL: BOY'S RIGHT FRONT JACKET PANEL

Assembling and Finishing the Jacket

1. Pin the front panels to the back RST; stitch at the shoulders. Serge or clean-finish the seams; press (see "Clean Finishing/Serging" on page 12).

2. Open each sleeve seam a few inches from the armpit so that you can easily insert the sleeves back into the armholes. Stitch the fronts and back together along the side seams, beginning at the bottom edge. Make sure to match the flannel seams, and continue up the side to join the original sleeve seam. Serge and press these key seams.

3. Gently round the front neck and bottom with a plate or dressmaker's curve. Refer to the photos on page 88 for guidance.

4. Cut 2 flannel binding strips 1½" wide. Piece the binding into one continuous strip. Attach it to the jacket edge for a crisp finish (see "Making and Attaching Binding" on pages 14–15).

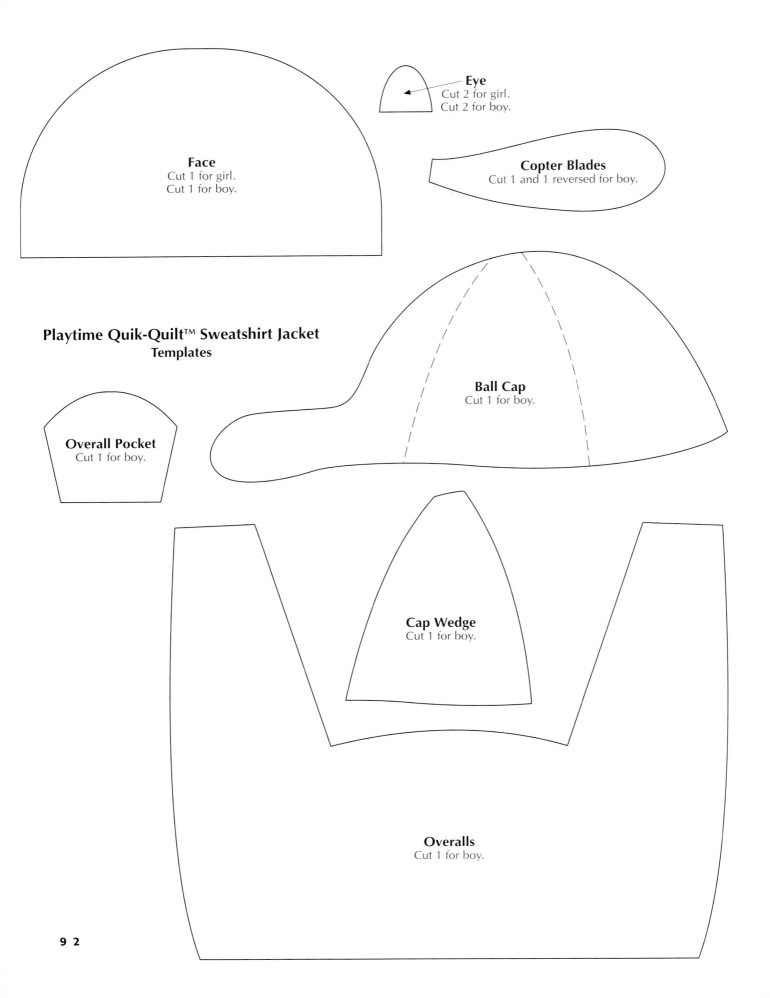

Face
Cut 1 for girl.
Cut 1 for boy.

Eye
Cut 2 for girl.
Cut 2 for boy.

Copter Blades
Cut 1 and 1 reversed for boy.

Playtime Quik-Quilt™ Sweatshirt Jacket
Templates

Ball Cap
Cut 1 for boy.

Overall Pocket
Cut 1 for boy.

Cap Wedge
Cut 1 for boy.

Overalls
Cut 1 for boy.

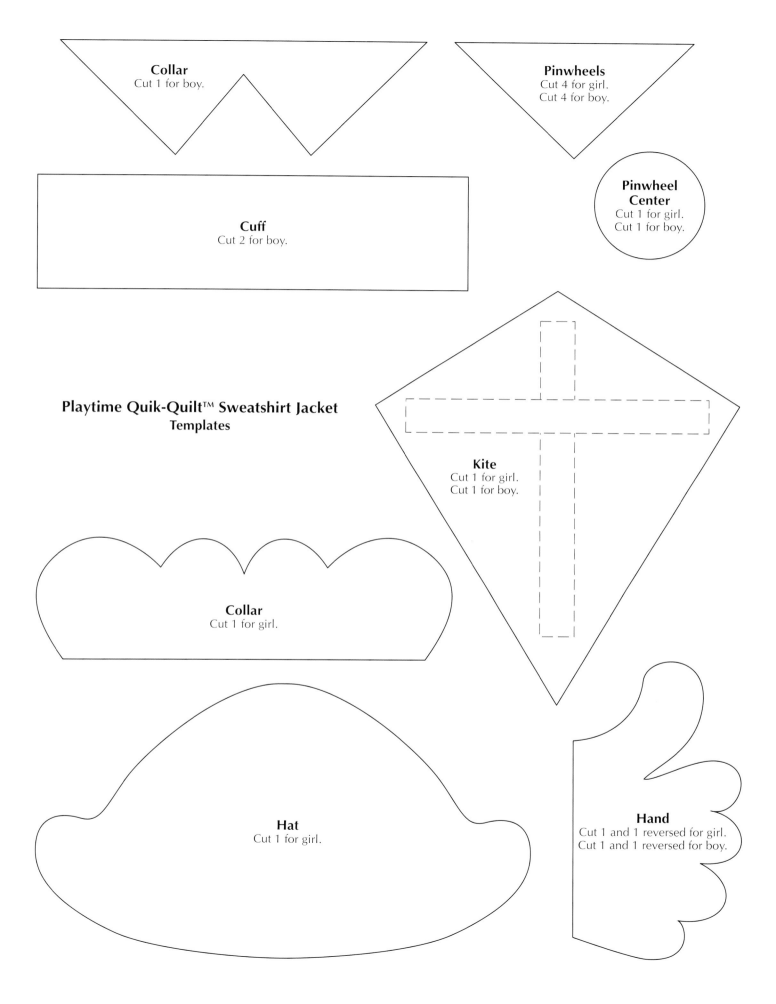

Collar
Cut 1 for boy.

Pinwheels
Cut 4 for girl.
Cut 4 for boy.

Cuff
Cut 2 for boy.

Pinwheel Center
Cut 1 for girl.
Cut 1 for boy.

Playtime Quik-Quilt™ Sweatshirt Jacket Templates

Kite
Cut 1 for girl.
Cut 1 for boy.

Collar
Cut 1 for girl.

Hat
Cut 1 for girl.

Hand
Cut 1 and 1 reversed for girl.
Cut 1 and 1 reversed for boy.

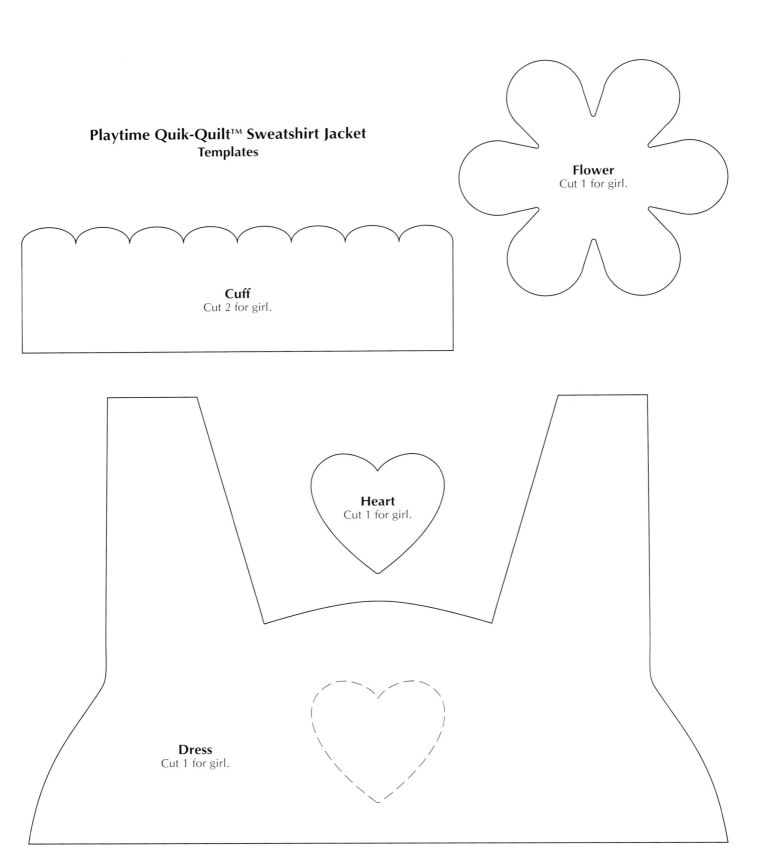

Playtime Quik-Quilt™ Sweatshirt Jacket
Templates

Flower
Cut 1 for girl.

Cuff
Cut 2 for girl.

Heart
Cut 1 for girl.

Dress
Cut 1 for girl.

RESOURCES

Cotton Way
495 North 4154 E
Rigby, ID 83442
Phone: 208-745-6742
Rag fringe

Kunin Felt
PO Box 5000
Hampton, NH 03843
Phone: 603-929-6100 (call for a store near you)
Web: www.kuninfelt.com
Rainbow™ washable craft felt, Shaggy plush felt, plush felt

Threadbare Pattern Co.
PO Box 1484
Havelock, NC 28532
Phone: 252-447-4081
Web: www.threadbarepatterns.com
Porcelain buttons

The Warm Company
954 East Union Street
Seattle, WA 98122
Phone: 206-320-9276
Web: www.warmcompany.com
Warm & Natural cotton batting, Steam-A-Seam 2 fusible webbing

Reproduction, fleece, and flannel fabrics are available at most local quilt stores. Check your local listings or the many Web sites offered on the Internet.

ABOUT THE AUTHOR

Cheryl Reinhard Jukich has been sewing whimsical clothing since Barbie dolls made their appearance. (Now try and guess her age!) She is well known for the embellished pattern line she designs for her company, Threadbare Patterns.

Cheryl resides with her husband, Bill, in the small town of Havelock, North Carolina, where hurricanes often stop for a visit. She has two grown children who can't sew on a button! But there is hope . . . she has a seven-year-old granddaughter (Emily, shown here) who is showing great promise.